C000088378

Living Beauty

Living Beauty

Ways of Mystical Prayer

OLIVER DAVIES

Darton, Longman and Todd
London

First published in 1990 by
Darton, Longman and Todd Ltd
89 Lillie Road, London SW6 1UD

British Library Cataloguing in Publication Data

Davies, Oliver
  Living beauty.
  1. Christian life – Devotional works
  I. Title
  242

ISBN 0–232–51858–0

The cover design features a detail from the Benjamin Britten Memorial
Window by John Piper, in Aldeburgh Parish Church, Suffolk. Used
by permission of the artist.

Phototypeset by Input Typesetting Ltd, London SW19 8DR
Printed and bound in Great Britain by
Courier International Ltd, Tiptree, Essex

Ei harddwch ái degwch, mewn cariad a hedd,
Anfeidrol ogoniant serchogrwydd ei wedd,
Ái ras at bechadur, penetwyn y tân,
Yw bywyd fy ysbryd a thestun fy nghân.
(Thomas Jones o Ddinbych, 1799)

I Rowan, Jane a Rhiannon

His beauty and his splendour, in love and in peace,
The glory immortal of the loveliness of his face,
His grace to the sinner, a flaming brand of fire,
Are the life of my spirit and subject of my song.
(Thomas Jones of Denbigh, 1799)

For Rowan, Jane and Rhiannon

Contents

Acknowledgements

The Scripture quotations in this publication are from the Revised Standard Version of the Bible, copyrighted 1971 and 1952 by the Division of Christian Education of the National Council of the Churches of Christ in the USA.

Preface

Paradoxically, this book feels to have been written from the
strength of my own shortcomings. Equally paradoxically, it
is a deeply personal book which lives from its debt to the
lives and works of others. It is in any case a book which
seeks to explore the more hidden areas of Christian living
and, as such, it is intended for those who wish to say Yes
to God in this way and to enter more deeply into these
mysteries.

The 'beauty' of God, which is the theme of this book, is
the special contribution to the Church which the great
Swiss theologian Hans Urs von Balthasar has made. And
it is a challenging theme which resonates widely in the
writings of the mystics of the past and those of today.
Above all, it reflects the experience which so many today
have, of the harmony and the gracefulness of a Christian
life, lived for others, in a world which is so often alienated,
disordered and in decay.

Living Beauty is a book which can be read privately, for
personal meditation, or in groups together. It can, I hope,
serve as a focus for a deeper meditation on the ways in
which we struggle to live a Christian life and on the ways
in which God draws us to do so.

A final word of thanks: above all to those many anonymous
people who have proved such an inspiration and who con-

tinue to do so. Here I would mention also the people of the new movements of the Church, such as l'Arche and the Focolare. Particular thanks are due to Bill Broderick, to Donald Allchin and to my wife, Fiona Bowie, for making valuable comments on the manuscript at a critical stage. I would also like to thank most warmly the staff of Darton, Longman and Todd for their work on the text, and in particular Sarah Baird-Smith, to whom this book owes a very real debt.

OLIVER DAVIES

The Inner Room

This is a book about spiritual beauty: that most special and precious beauty which is of the inner life and the spirit. Beauty is a splendid thing. Think of all that we find beautiful: a marvellous dawn or sunset, a sudden view which lifts the heart and fills us with fresh, cleansing emotions, the subtle beauty of music or a work of art, the vital beauty of animals or people, of landscape or even machines. And yet this kind of beauty is as nothing compared with that beauty which is of the spirit, which seems to emerge from within, casting light all around. This is the beauty of Christ himself, which was constant and bright even when he suffered all the savagery the human race is capable of: all our indifference, our viciousness, our barbarity. Even on the cross, above all on the cross, Jesus is the supremely Beautiful One, who transcends the most appalling conditions of our human reality through his loving assent to the will of the Father. In him, in the face of and even precisely through his torment and his suffering, we see the radiance of holiness, the fragrance of a pure life, the light and fire of a transforming love.

That is the kind of beauty which this book is about. A spiritual beauty which both satisfies us and makes us yearn for more, so much so that, with St Augustine, we pull and stretch our hearts so that they may contain even more. It is a beauty which is the meaning of the world, but constantly leads us beyond it. It is a beauty which makes us die to our old self and live to the new, grace-filled person we slowly become.

In order to explore this idea of beauty, I want to begin by taking you on a journey. A journey within yourself. I want you to see a place deep within you, at the very core of your being. There is a room there. The air is very still, for no turbulence disturbs it. It is deep, far too deep, to be affected by the moods and uncertainties of our everyday living. This room is at the very heart of what we *are*, and is unmoved in silence and stillness.

Enter this room now. Imagine yourself descending to it, going deeper and deeper. Go as deep as you can and then feel yourself there, in this silent room at the very centre, the very ground, of your being.

Now this room is holy. God is present here. Feel him. Feel the sanctity of his presence, uplifting, purifying, bathing you in the fragrance of his holiness. This is the heart-room, for God and for you; it is the room of Truth. Here we are in the presence of the Almighty.

There is a high window in this room: look at it now. It is a brightly coloured window that fills the far wall. Many different colours are there, many different contours and shapes. But one thing unites them all: the light. Behind this window there is a bright source of light that falls upon it. It is the light which brings it to life, for without it everything would be colourless and dead. It is the light that makes it beautiful, picking out the colours and shapes, purifying them and making them exact.

Now this window is our life, and the light that shines through it is the abundant grace of God. All living creatures partake of that grace, whether they know it or not. The light shines equally upon all windows, but not all windows

2

are able to receive that light equally: to become transparent, alive, brilliant and of supernatural beauty.

So let us look at our own window, which is the pattern of our own living. If it seems static, that is because change here, at this deep level, happens only slowly. This is the place of the deepest reality. See the many colours of our window: are they pure, clear, radiant colours? Or are there areas of darkness and dullness? See the light that suffuses the window, seeming to illumine it from within. Is this not a heavenly light? Is it not the light that we desire, hunger for even?

Now we will take each and every colour in the window and we will follow it back to the surface: to the reality of our everyday existence in the world. In this way we may discover the particular picture which our own life represents: its areas of ugliness or resistance to the light, or of indifference to it. And we shall by grace discover the presence of God in our lives, the supremely Beautiful One, who transforms all that we are in the radiant glory of his being – if only we let him.

1

The Prayer of Silence

Our quest for beauty begins with the question: What place does silence have in the world we have made for ourselves? Everywhere and at all times, it seems, we are surrounded by noise: the noise of telephones ringing, of traffic, of aeroplanes, the noise of radios and television sets. Silence, which is surely the natural state, has been pushed to the margins to such an extent that we need to struggle for it, to insist upon it, and, for some people when it comes upon them suddenly, silence can even seem quite alien and strange.

What is at the heart of this noise which is everywhere so prevalent is that ours is a culture of 'doing'. We seem to live in a society which is a vast organism in which everyone engages with everyone else. In our daily work we are constantly being asked to perform, to do things, to respond to requests, to reply. Rarely, it seems, if ever, is there an opportunity simply to *be*. To stand outside the interconnecting pathways of constant movement, to practise silence and simply to be.

And, of course, we all know what the consequence of this imbalance is. When our energies are constantly directed outwards, how quickly our inner and private world becomes desiccated and barren. We are like our own bodies in this. When we use our muscles in physical activity, then this is like our own 'doing', and when finally we rest them and recuperate, then this is like our 'being'. While it is good to exercise the muscles, and indeed it is essential to their well-being, if we do not constantly replenish them with nourishment, then they will need to draw upon the resources of the body itself, first fat tissue and then muscle tissue, in order to continue to perform. If denied rest and replenishment for long enough, then our muscles will finally begin to devour themselves. And is this not just how it feels for us when our 'doing' far outweighs our 'being'? We find then that we no longer have the energy and inner resources to feed our actions; rather, they seem to destroy us in some way, to eat into the fabric of our own being. And so a culture such as the one in which we live, which is based not so much upon the simplicity of what we 'are' as on what we can 'achieve', on our 'performance', can often demand too much of us. Rather than feeling fulfilled and invigorated by our actions, we begin to feel ultimately that we are reduced and diminished by what we do. And so if we are to live healthy physical and spiritual lives, then we need to correct the imbalance which life too often imposes upon us. And, if a proper and wholesome balance is to be maintained between our 'being' and our 'doing', then we must find periods and places in our lives in which we are no longer constrained always to 'do' but can allow ourselves simply to 'be'.

Jesus himself sought this balance too. Mark (1:35) tells us how after healing many sick people from the surrounding area, Jesus rose early in the morning 'a great while before day' and went out to 'a lonely place' in order to pray. He sought the stillness of the desert in order to balance the activity of the previous day. He sought the silence of God in order to understand more deeply his mission on earth (1:38) and what God's will for him was. And yet even for him, this period of silence did not last long, for soon 'Simon

6

and those who were with him followed him, and they found him' (1:36–37). In fact, the Greek word which Mark uses here is *katadioko*, which could almost be translated as 'they hunted him down'! And so – like Jesus – we must seek our own 'lonely place' where we can speak to God in the silence, free from all the demands of other people, although perhaps – as was the case for Jesus – our silence will all too soon be disturbed by the calling of familiar voices!

The desire for silence is the beginning of prayer. Our life can so often be a broken thing. Despite our best intentions, our experience in the world often serves to distract us from the things that really matter, abandoning us to triviality, to foolishness and banality. Even if we set out at the beginning of the day full of good intentions to love God in all things and to show his love to others, the wear and tear of our daily living can easily lead us to lose touch with this commitment. And so we snap back, when we had hoped to be calm and restrained. We spend our time in useless chatter, when we had hoped to be collected within. We scowl and we sulk, when we had wished to be radiant with God's love. The truth is that we easily become fragmented and alienated from our own true selves. Prayer, then, the prayer of silence, is the place where we are made whole again. In prayer we are renewed, and returned to ourselves. Through prayer we become centred in God, and are restored to the meaning, simplicity and coherence of our own being. Prayer is a re-gathering of the self, of the whole, and is a kind of resting in God, which renews our powers and returns us to ourselves.

One of the worst ways in which we disturb the silence is by the sound of our own voice. It is not speaking that is wrong, for it is often right to speak so that true and beautiful things can be said. The problem is that so often we say the things we should not say, or we gossip, and gossip soon turns to backbiting. We find that with our tongue 'we bless the Lord and Father, and with it we curse men, who are made in the likeness of God. From the same mouth come blessing and cursing' (James 3:9–10). Somehow our tongue thwarts our intentions. Although we do not mean to speak ill of people, that is what we do, and when we should be maintaining silence, we speak flippantly or out of turn. Thomas à Kempis captures this exactly when he says: 'Flee the tumult of men as much as you can, for the talk of worldly affairs is a great hindrance, although they are discussed with sincere intention. For we are quickly defiled and enthralled with vanity. Often I could wish that I had held my peace, and that I had not been among men.' And so we must cultivate silence. We must let silence itself govern our mouth and form our speech, not so that we are always silent, but in order that the calmness and correctness of the silence shall be reflected in the words we speak. As the Epistle of James reminds us: 'The tongue is a fire' and 'how great a forest is set ablaze by a small fire!' (James 3:6, 5).

The desire for silence is the beginning of prayer. And there are many different ways of praying, perhaps as many as there are different kinds of person. We hear a good deal these days about the techniques of prayer, almost as if it were something that can be learned. But prayer is not a method to be mastered; it is a gift to be received. 'Learning' to pray is the process of learning to recognize a great and astonishing gift which God gives us all: the gift of a special kind of speech, a special kind of being, which is quite different from any other.

Prayer needs silence.

God speaks with a 'still, small voice'. He moves us gently, in general, from within with a quiet voice that we must learn to discern among all the distractions of a hundred other 'voices'. It is no use waiting for God to switch all the other sounds off and to bellow in our ear. Of course, he might do just that. But we will be foolish to count on it.

And so the prayer of silence begins with the act of listening. Listening to God's voice, as it sounds within us. Now, some of the noise which threatens to drown it out will have an external source: the television is on, someone is speaking to me, there are noises on the street outside, people shouting, lorries roaring. It is only natural that as we seek to 'tune in' to God's quiet, inward speech, we will seek to exclude all forms of exterior distraction. We will switch the television off; retire to our own room; go away, perhaps, on retreat to a place where silence is valued and safeguarded. That is the first stage in dimming exterior noise, voices which are not God's voice: reaching for silence.

Silence is a precious thing. It allows us to be, rather than to do. It lets us sink within ourselves and be restored. It opens up to us a great wealth of the interior life. And yet silence is a far deeper thing than the absence of exterior noise, which is only its beginning. True silence is a silence within. How many voices are there going on in our heads at any one time? Conversations between different parts of ourselves: emergent desires, incomplete thoughts? All this disturbs the silence of the spirit and distracts us. Perhaps there are even squabbles between these different voices, clashing opinions, tensions that raise the blood pressure, so the overall effect is one of noise, of cacophony. We will be little served by exterior silence if we carry within us the noises of the busiest London street. And so we must take a further step.

The beginning of silence is the act of listening, and the fulfilment of silence is the act of letting go. Letting go all those things, no matter what they are, which trouble us and which buzz around in our heads with the persistence of bees. Of course, some distractions are better solved on the spot (did I pay that bill? Have I left the hotplate on?), but most cannot be dealt with in the present moment; they need to be let go. Letting go, paradoxically, is a discipline. We need to train ourselves in it. We get used so quickly to hanging on to things, straining with them. Such behaviour can be appropriate in many of life's situations, as we go about our daily business and have to react in the right way to what is going on around us. This preoccupation is not wrong, then, in itself, it is only inappropriate as we approach a deepening silence; it gets in the way. And so we need to learn the habit of letting go, of trusting things to the silence, of allowing ourselves to sink into the silence, the 'darkness of soundlessness', and away from those murmuring, chattering, squabbling voices that hold us back.

The prayer of silence is a prayer which takes us away from the world with all its distractions into that secret and hidden place which is at the heart of us all. There we meet God, who moves as an unseen Presence in that darkness and yet who is 'closer to me than I am to myself' (St Augustine). Silence in this sense is a place of encounter at the deepest level of our being. It is where we come closest to God and learn to know him, discovering him as an infinite point at the very centre of our being.

Silence is the heart of prayer.

And the heart of silence is transformation. That silence which comes upon us as a discovery, as a gift from God, is in fact the place of our transformation. We are transformed by silence; changed into something new. Although in truth, of course, it is not silence that transforms us but God. For silence is the garment that God wears when he comes to us in this special, most intimate way. It is God's apparel. And, as he draws close to us, we realize that this

10

garment of silence is a mantle of fire. Silence is transforming fire which draws us into itself, burning and consuming what is impure. It is primal Divine Fire which renews us, which destroys us and brings us to life again.

Three things need to be said about this prayer of silence. The first is that there are some for whom it seems an alien thing. And how easy it is to say: No, God does not come to me in that way. I am not that type of person. God does not choose to come to me like that. And yet the truth is that it is *we* who do not want God to come to us in this most special way. For why should the Father withhold himself, if we desire him truly? Surely he stands constantly at our side, waiting for the chance, the right moment, to take possession of us: to lay claim to our inner being with his love and his presence. It is we who keep him at bay, by our distractions and preoccupations, by our own divided will, when at any moment he wills to come to us, to possess us and make us his own. And so we should learn submission, if we will know him truly and as he wishes himself to be known. We should allow him to work upon us with his beauty as the sun melts hardened ice. For in the end no one and no thing in all creation can resist him. Not even us.

Prayer, then, the prayer of silence, is something for us all. We would be wrong to think of it as something special, for those in religious houses, perhaps: the chosen few. We are all chosen. We are all called. Now the second question which arises is this: What should I do, then: how do I pray?

There are of course many books available which tell us how to pray. Some of these are useful, but at the same time they may make us feel that there is something we should know about prayer if we are to do it right; some information others have, perhaps, but not us. That is the danger of

11

writing books on prayer. They encourage us to think that prayer is something we *do* rather than something we *are*. The best books on prayer are those which make us feel that we *want* to pray. For the desire to pray is itself the beginning of prayer.

A useful analogy here is that of falling in love (an experience which most of us will have had at some time!). Now love is not something we do but something we feel, ultimately something we *are* towards another person. There are no techniques for falling in love any more than there are for *being* in love. Love just happens, and it draws us along its own path. We wish to spend time with the beloved, to share with the beloved, to grow into the beloved so that we have a common life.

Now it is the same with God and our life of prayer. Prayer is our love-affair with God; it is our courtship and the time we spend with him. It is our desiring him and longing for him. How many hours and minutes we can find each day to sit silently in prayer is not so important, therefore; it does not matter so much what we do. What is important, rather, is what we are, for God. Whether we want him and tell him so. Whether we seek him and, even though we may be occupied with our daily work at the time, ask him to be with us. Prayer is a motion of the heart, a reaching out to God. It is a cry, a movement, a caress, even a taste when we experience what some mystics have called the sweetness of God. And so we should not ask ourselves: am I doing it right? or have any vague sense of bad conscience about neglected duty. The questions we should ask ourselves are: Do I love God in this moment, *now*? Am I being faithful to him (as I should be to those I love)? Once this is right, when we stand before him in love, then we will know well enough when and how we should pray. Lovers find time to be together!

12

But, of course, it is not always like this. Just as human lovers go through periods of difficulty, we too, God's lovers, come into times of dryness. And yet we should not be too hard on ourselves here. There have been times when I have heard people talk of their failure to love when it has been quite clear that they have been under great pressure of some kind. They are tired, under stress at work, they are feeling weak, misunderstood, or exploited. There are times when all of us feel this way, and then our love-affair with God grows cold. We may go through lengthy periods when it feels as if God has withdrawn from us completely or that we have simply lost interest in him and are not free to do anything about it. We are surrounded by failure. The causes of such a period can be various. It may be that we are going through a time of strain in general in our lives, overworked or excessively burdened in some way that robs us of our inner peace and stability. And if we are hard upon ourselves and judgemental at this point, then the situation will only become worse. We can easily become embittered towards a world which seems to take so little account of what we are, and of what our own special needs are. How easy it is to take the view then that life is an exercise in survival in which no quarter is given or taken. And worse: If we have to stamp on our own needs and nature in the face of the reality of our life, our job, our family, then why should we have regard for the specialness of other people's needs? We may easily feel that they are in a battle for survival too, in which they will sink or swim, and that it is a question of everyone for themselves. We have all seen those sad members of society who have over-come great difficulties in their own lives through courage and strength of character and yet who feel that since this was their lot, it should be everyone else's too. It is often those who have themselves survived poverty who are most vindictive and unfeeling towards the poor, when this experience should bring understanding and compassion. Such feelings are natural and understandable, and all of us at some time will experience them. But they are dangerous, for they undermine our life in God and our own humanity.

When we experience failure in our spiritual life, therefore, we should realize that it is paradoxically our strength. The worst thing of all is when we become spiritually self-satisfied. Complacency is an insuperable wall between ourselves and God; it blocks him off and surrounds us with an impenetrable air of self-absorption and unreality. Failure is altogether a healthier state to be in since it reminds us as powerfully as anything can that we are in our spiritual life, as in all things, entirely dependent upon God and his grace. He leads us, he is our light, our strength and our guide, and without him all movement is impossible – except backwards.

Failure in prayer, then, is failure at the level of the heart, and is a failure in love. It is here, therefore, at the very centre of our being, that the problem must be addressed and solved. This is what Meister Eckhart means when he says: 'You will find God again there where you left him.' In one sense God is a heavenly, transcendent Being, a point beyond our experience to which our life and being is directed as to its ultimate end. This God is easily lost hold of: we need only slip or stumble to lose this high vision of him and to be faced by the (sometimes pitiless) world of our daily living: the reality of hunger and frustration, of worry and fear, the swings of mood, irritation and depression. When this happens, then we must learn to know God in a new way. We must learn to know him as the Incarnate Son who shares our human reality with us, while retaining his divine nature in all its fullness. This is a very different

14

face of God: it is God seen in shadows, in half-understood truths, in despair. It is the God of the half-light, of the wounded light, the God of that sinking moment when things go out of control, when we are abandoned to the whims of others, to the arbitrariness of situation or the compulsions of our own nature. This is God as he is in his human and divine truth.

The starting-point for the God of this kind is not some remote Heaven to which we can aspire, but is the human place we inhabit now, ourselves, in this very moment. God remains with us however far we sink, however trivial we become, however great our failure. He is there in the fullest and most real sense where we may feel him to be absent. And so, when it seems to us that we have lost him, the important thing is that we do not simply give up and assume we have in some way failed an important and unrepeatable exam. We should not simply reject our present experience of dryness as being an irrelevant, meaningless and unavoidable aspect of our lives. Rather, we must embrace that despair as being in some mysterious way part of God's presence to us. We must acknowledge him in us, within the present situation, our present experience, and learn to discern the features of the God who suffers, who, on the cross, loses orientation and the sense of his own divine transcendence, who suffered, died and was buried. In this way, by not turning from the reality in which we find ourselves but by embracing it as a form of God's presence to us, we shall come to share in God's suffering. And by sharing his suffering, we can be certain that we shall share his resurrection into light.

Living Beauty

QUESTIONS TO ASK OURSELVES

1 Is there enough silence in my life?

2 Do I make use of the silence that there is in the right way? Or do I turn the television or radio on when I could spend a few minutes in prayer?

3 Do I escape from myself and from God by hiding in the cacophony of life and a never-ending doing?

4 Am I sufficiently aware of periods of failure in my prayer life, and is this a failure to love?

5 Do I sometimes yield to despair in my spiritual life, when I should turn to God for help?

6 Can I say that I have a love-affair with God? Do I look forward to spending time with him as I would with a human lover?

7 Is God the fullness, the meaning and the end of my existence?

2

The Prayer of Freedom

The Book of Genesis begins: 'In the beginning God created
the heavens and the earth.' God wills the world in which
we live. And the light that shines upon the window at the
centre of our being, illumining every colour and contour of
our lives, is the will of God. This is the divine reality
which surrounds us on all sides. It is the divine presence
everywhere and at all times. God, by his will, sustains all
creatures in life. The whole of creation speaks of his will
that these things should be, that life and world should be,
that we should be. God wills each moment and each thing.
And he wills above all that we should be free.

But how difficult freedom can be.

There are many signs of our 'freedom' today. There is
our freedom with respect to the world of which we are a
part, for instance. The freedom to take from it more than
it can give. The freedom to pollute the earth, to con-
taminate it for centuries with the dangerous dross of our
civilization and to expose it to a real threat of massive
environmental destruction. All this in order to serve the
short-term, short-sighted aims of minimum expenditure.
There is the freedom to threaten the planet with definitive
and total destruction on the grounds of what often seems
no more than national one-upmanship. There is the freedom we possess to set up the grotesque idol of the profit
motive, which demands that all human and environmental

interests shall be finally subordinated to the one overriding principle of cash in hand.

And we are free also with regard to our fellow human beings. We have the freedom to exploit the poor (once again in the name of profit), to oppress those who are different, or weak. We are free to ignore those in our society with special needs, with mental or physical handicap, and to marginalize them. We are free to let the disadvantaged fend for themselves, in the belief that only the strong should survive. We are free to let the hungry starve.

And you and I are free, too, to say that this is no concern of ours, to confine ourselves to our own small world. We are free to harbour unspoken prejudice against others, to quarrel with our neighbour through over-zealous defence of our rights. We are free to be patronizing or indifferent to those who need our help. We are free to fail in our ideals and our aims, and to condemn others in their failure.

God created us free.

But here, too, we encounter paradox. After all, it is not freedom which lies at the root of these things; rather, what we see here is the loss of freedom. When we sin, we do not do so from the heart of our God-given freedom; but when we sin, we are in flight from freedom. We are turning our backs upon the true freedom in our lives and are embracing a life of servility: a way of being which is based upon the compulsions of our appetites, the deathly logic of our calculated self-interest, the blind stupidity which is all that remains when we refuse the option, the life-giving challenge, of taking up that freedom which God has given us and which remains as a presence or a potential at the heart of us all.

God made us free. He wills us to be free.

And yet, it seems, being free is one of the most difficult things we can do. It is something that has to be learned, often at considerable cost to ourselves, and once gained it must be retained with great vigilance and sometimes with courage. For freedom, the true, radical freedom which we have in God, is at the very heart of what we are, of what makes us human. If we do not take it up, then something integral within us will be permanently closed-off and unfulfilled. Our life will be a life half-lived and in shadows.

We often think of freedom simply as the capacity to choose. But real freedom is the depth-choice of God and of his way for us. It is the preparedness to live by his will and not our own. To follow his way, which leads to abundant self-giving life, and not the way of a personality closed in upon itself in which selfishness takes on innumerable forms which deaden and ossify. It is the heartfelt recognition that God in all his mystery and otherness leads us to our own truth and to a life that is authentic, beautiful and real. For the capacity for freedom within us, the ability to choose God above all, is itself something transcendental. It opens us up to the transformation of divine life. It takes us beyond ourselves and makes us a channel for the infinite goodness and beauty of the divine. When we are free, truly free in this way, then we are happy and light-hearted; we are fully alive. And we know joy.

But this kind of freedom is quite different from those other 'freedoms' which are sometimes proclaimed in our society and which in truth are forms of oppression, both of the self and of others. There is for instance the political clarion call of individual liberty above all, which seems to ignore those bonds of deeper interest which exist between us all on the basis of our common humanity. And this kind of 'freedom' can so easily turn into the oppression of the many by the few. If we believe in individual freedoms within society, then we must fight for the freedom of our fellow human beings too, with all that this entails, such

19

as proper housing, proper education and full equality of opportunity. We must understand that their freedom is our freedom, their well-being is our well-being. We need to judge political systems of whichever complexion on the basis of their valuing and caring for people, those people they so often claim to serve, and not as an idea but as a reality.

And there is a second type of freedom which is much spoken of today. This is the freedom of a humanistic rejection of God, which has its roots often in compassion. The French existentialist philosopher, Jean-Paul Sartre, represents for many the idea that it is the rejection of religion which represents the greatest act of human freedom. And in his novel *La Peste* (*The Plague*), Albert Camus makes one of his characters say: 'I shall never accept a creation in which innocent children suffer.' There is much that is good in the very real sense of sorrow and outrage that many people feel who hold this view. But it is not the Christian path. For us to reject the seemingly meaningless suffering of both the good and the innocent in this world is, at the same time, for us to reject Christ. Though infinitely gentle, innocent and good, Christ died a terrible death upon the cross. For us who follow him, all human suffering happens in the light of that sacrifice, and though such suffering confounds our natural reason and sense of justice, it is a place in which God in Christ is peculiarly present to us. He calls us not away from this mystery but to go with him into its very heart. And though, as the poet Saunders Lewis says, we enter 'silent into the mystery', it is there, paradoxically and miraculously, that we find the truest liberty.

But if freedom in Christ, who died for us and rose again, is the ultimate truth of our existence, which knows so much of suffering, then it is also true that it is the greatest

20

challenge. And how often true freedom, which is discipleship in Christ, evades us! It is all too familiar as an ideal but all too rare as a reality. And what blocks us and prevents us from taking up our inheritance is that most implacable of opponents: ourself. No one and no thing can stop us being free but we ourselves. And at times it seems to us that choosing freedom, choosing to live a life of spiritual beauty, is the most difficult thing in all the world: it is as impossible as jumping to the moon. We are weighed down, we cannot move, with the great burden of all our acquired characteristics, all our habits of mind, our habitual responses and defences so that rather than being full of light, movement and air, as freedom requires, we feel that we are so heavily burdened we can scarcely crawl! All our hopes and best intentions can be instantly scattered by the chill wind that blows from the past: from our old habits, our old self. What point is there in trying to live life differently, in a light newness of being, when we carry around with us all the time the lead-lined overcoat of our past mistakes, grudges, irritations and general human 'mess'?

The answer is this: there is no point at all. Until we shed that overcoat, all our endeavours will be in vain. And they will be in vain precisely because they are *our* endeavours, our striving, our struggle. The reality is that, though this freedom, which is the freedom of the highest kind, is the easiest thing in all the world to achieve, it is not we who can achieve it, for it is permanently and emphatically beyond our powers. God alone can work that freedom in us, and for him it is quite the easiest task of all. What we need to do, then, is *ask him* to do for us what we cannot do for ourselves. We need to vacate the scene, to disappear so that he can come and achieve what he alone can achieve.

21

In the words of one medieval preacher, John Tauler, 'We do not need to learn how to *do* but how *not* to do'.

Now, of course, learning not to do can be far more difficult than learning to do. What is required here is a kind of inner denuding of self, an internal poverty, which can be likened to the construction of a landing-strip. If God is to land within us, then everything must first be cleared away which is likely to obstruct him. Even a relatively small thing, such as an area of possessiveness in us or a nagging resistance to God's will, can block his passage. Our task is to chop down the trees and clear the undergrowth of our own particular 'mess' so that a clearing can open up for him, an inner space.

But how are we to 'do' this which, by its very nature, cannot be 'done', at least not by us? The answer is that we need to look deep within ourselves to where we become mysterious even to ourselves. We need to seek out that deepest area within us which is our own essential *will*. It is this which can become the door through which God enters us, if only we let him. Our own will, stubborn and obstinate though it may be, can become an altar for him. And this means the willingness to allow him to use us as he will, to take us up into his, far greater, reality. To allow ourselves (precious though we may be in our own eyes!) to be consumed as a burnt-offering to him.

In Isaiah 55:8 we read: 'For my thoughts are not your thoughts, neither are your ways my ways, says the Lord', and it is the difference between the ways of God and our own ways which is this place of sacrifice. In the darkness of faith Abraham leads his son Isaac out into the wilderness in order to sacrifice him, until God sends the ram, caught in the bush. This is the obedience which we must learn in our own lives in a thousand different ways. But it is not easily done. In fact it can be one of the most difficult things

22

of all to do. Our nature fights back, in moments of difficulty our hurt and our fear seem immediate and strong, our resistance is tenacious and deeply-rooted. But in the midst of all this misery, there is still something we can do: we can say Yes to God in loving acceptance of his will. And then say Yes again.

This path of acceptance is the only path we can follow in order to be emptied of all things, and to be emptied of them in such a way that we may be filled with God. For anything else just makes our will struggle rather than allowing it to yield simply to God's infinitely greater and truer will, and thus can only lead to a yet greater 'mess'. The precious gift which God has given us and which is all we need for his plan to come to fruition in us is the acceptance of his will for us in the present moment: 'Thy will be done, not mine.' It is in these words of Jesus that we find the highest point of human submission to the divine. If we wish to follow him, then this is the message that we must learn, and make actual in our own lives, not once but a thousand times. God asks nothing else of us, and there is nothing else that we can give.

The uncontrolled 'mess' of our inner lives happens precisely when it is we who are in charge and not God; when, like St Paul, we intend good and do evil. When we hurt in some way those we love; when we encourage in our lives what we most detest. This 'mess' is where we fail in our own best intentions, and in this failure are made to feel impotent: it is the absurd and seemingly irredeemable situation of feeling angry and frustrated with ourselves for feeling angry and frustrated yet again. This is the condition in which, to a greater or lesser extent, we all live, and it is the area in which we need to learn true poverty of will. The root cause of the problem of 'mess' is the suffering struggle of our own will to put things right when all that

23

we do leads to failure. That is its peculiar characteristic; 'mess' is always in some way self-inflicted. The answer in this situation is not to struggle on, carrying ourselves on our backs like a heavy weight that drags us down; rather, the answer is to release the tension that is at the root of the problem and which is we ourselves: the pulling, tugging energy of will. And this is why, when confronted by the implacable opposition of our own nature, when in times of trial and difficulty, we need to say silently to ourselves: 'Father, thy will be done.' We need consciously to withdraw from the situation and to allow God to take over. In this way, and in this way alone, we will find peace and relief, and the problem will vanish like morning mist in a bright sun.

And there is something else we should notice about our 'mess'. It is not something which life imposes upon us from time to time; rather, it is something which we carry with ourselves, like a sore thumb or neck. As we advance through the changing circumstances of our daily living, life serves time and again to highlight the problem: just as with a sore thumb or neck, every other movement seems to jar us with pain. And although, when we have a sore thumb, we know full well that the problem is in us, when it comes to our own 'mess', we are not so sure. How easy it is to assume that every time we 'fail' in our own particular ways, the fault lies not with us but with the world. If we have a problem with losing our temper, then we may imagine that we are always surrounded by intolerable people. If we persistently feel misjudged and misunderstood, it may be that we are failing to recognize that we are misjudging and misunderstanding the response of others to ourselves. Many seemingly objective situations in life are actually the result of our own perceptions. As the Greek proverb puts it: one man looked out of his prison window and saw mud, the other saw the stars.

The essentially human truth is that this 'mess' is work that we still have to do before God: it is those parts of ourselves that we still need to integrate into our deeper, spiritual way of being. But not all is darkness here. For we can think of these difficult areas, although they can cause us so much frustration and pain, as the luminous areas of our lives: the spiritual front line. They are so because it is in them that we have the capacity to *grow into* God's will. We have the opportunity to say Yes to him: to receive him into the circumstances of our own lives and into the depths of our own being. And this saying Yes to him is to accept his transformation, which, however painful it may be (and it can be exceedingly painful!), is a good pain, the pain of growth, and is infinitely preferable to the deadly, suffocatingly dull complacency of No.

The will of God is a great, wonderful and deeply mysterious thing. Moreover, it is the way in which he makes himself present to us in the midst of our daily living. We can think of it as a path which runs through our lives and which we are invited to follow. Or as a light which guides us and leads us through the great variety of our existence, and which is the measure of all things. Now, part of the mystery of God's will is that it is something which knows no half-measures. To give our will to God is to give him all that we are, and have, and all that we shall ever be. It is a wholehearted action that accepts without reservation and makes no preconditions and sets no limits. Meister Eckhart is right when he says: 'He who has given up his will has given up all things.' In saying Yes to God, we are called to offer ourselves wholly to him, without reservation. We are called to open ourselves up to him unconditionally, from the heart of our being.

25

But of course this is not the end of the story. We are creatures who live in time, and no decision, however momentous it may feel in that moment, is invulnerable to the passage of time. Time sweeps all before it; it can turn the most heartfelt words into mere sounds that mean nothing. And so the choosing of God is not something that happens once and for all; rather, it is a continuous process. It is ongoing, like our life itself, and can on this earth have no end. We choose God now in this moment, and then in the next, and again in the next. In fact, our choosing of him becomes less an act in time than a way of being, as we place him, the good and the beautiful, first in our lives. But here too there is a place for paradox. For how easily we become complacent and too sure of ourselves, in this as in any other matter. The rhythms of daily life have a habit of breaking down any inner conviction by which we live. And so, if we are not to err, we must know that we do err; if we are not to fail God in this way, in the choosing of him in our lives, then we must know that we do fail him and that we fail him all the time!

It seems to us sometimes a surprising but nevertheless profound truth that God speaks to us most clearly in the ordinary and everyday circumstances of our lives. Indeed, if we turn away from the centre of our ordinary existence, thinking that God will only speak to us in grand and exceptional ways, then we may miss his voice altogether. God speaks to us in the here and now, in the reality which is ours, however humdrum and mundane that reality may seem to us who inhabit it twenty-four hours a day.

At the heart of every moment there is the question of God's will for us. But the will of God is not 'part' of the world as other things are; nor is it something which exists one moment and not the next. Rather, the will of God is like a light that shines constantly upon our existence from its greatest depths, illumining us at every moment and in every area of our experience. It is something we can never in any sense escape, although we can, of course, choose not to follow the direction of that light as it falls upon us. We can habitually or wilfully turn away from it, and so lose all sensitivity to it. But we can never wander so far that we move out of the range of that light, for it shines both from within the heart of our existence and from beyond it.

God has made us free, radically free, and to live within that freedom is to live from the centre of our being. This freedom leads us not out of the world, but directly into the world. It takes us into the reality of our own lives. For this is where God speaks to us living words. It is in our daily living that we grow towards him or away from him. It is here, in the circumstances of our everyday lives, that we refuse him or accept him. And to live from within this freedom, to have the courage to do so, is at the same time to live a great open-ended adventure.

For God is great. And to choose to live in openness to him, to commit ourselves radically and unreservedly to follow him wherever he may lead us, is in a sense to be born again. It is to emerge from the old world into a new reality. And this new freedom of ours, to which we can now lay claim, is a mighty thing. Like the great phenomena of Nature that dwarf us, it shocks us out of all our past certainties and complacency of spirit and brings us into a new realm of *possibility*. Sometimes the will of God may seem gentle to us, a 'still, small voice' (1 Kings 19:12), a voice like a breeze, but sometimes it may be like the advent of a powerful angel or messenger of God. Then, like Zacharias in the holy of holies or like Mary herself in the annunciation, we find ourselves suddenly confronted with an event which transcends our understanding but which demands our absolute assent and obedience. This is the 'angel' moment in life when we suddenly perceive that God is speaking to us, with words of fire, from the root of our lived experience. The event may be of any kind: the death of a loved one, a threat to our own physical being, or it may be something entirely personal and individual which no one else knows anything about. But when such 'angel' moments occur, we know then that we are in the presence of the living God. And we are shaken to the core! We feel that we are surrounded by an 'abyss', as John Tauler says, and are filled with the rush of fear which comes from this sudden contact with another, infinitely greater order of reality. Such 'angel' moments befall us all at some time or another, and remain in the memory for a long time as fertile, focal points of our existence. And though they make us tremble, such moments are good, for they are essentially *true*. And they are a form of truth upon which we may found our lives. For though the God who is himself the source of life, may at times enter our lives as a strange, vast and awesome Being, he brings not death but only more and deeper life.

The choice of freedom is the choice of a life that is true, beautiful and good. That has been the theme of this chapter. And by accepting the will of God in our own lives, we become a path for God to walk into the midst of the world. Through living in his Spirit, our lives take on the beauty which is his, and thus we can become, in and through his power, a source of beauty for all the world.

QUESTIONS TO ASK OURSELVES

1   Do I accept the challenge of God's gift of freedom to me?

28

2   Do I run away from my own freedom, through fear, scepticism or indifference?

3   Do I allow myself to become enslaved in little ways 'that do not matter': through smoking or drinking, through bad habits, habitual and unthinking responses, through closed areas of my life ('my little vices') in which I push God aside?

4   Do I accept where I am now (despite all its 'mess') as being a place in which God speaks directly to me?

5   Do I say Yes to God, and am I prepared to let him make of my life a channel for his beauty: a window upon heaven?

6   Am I someone who experiences 'angels'? Do I recognize the presence of God when he touches me or my life in a special way?

7   Do I choose God fully now, in this present moment of time?

3

The Prayer of Powerlessness

I shall certainly never forget one thing that happened to me when I was a small child at school. We were sitting as a class in the school hall, waiting for a physical education lesson, when the teacher pointed at me and said: 'You, boy, move the form.' Now, of course, what the teacher meant by this was: 'You, boy, move the bench' (there was a bench nearby). I leaped to my feet instantly and then stood in a state of paralysis. I had never heard the word 'form' in this sense before, and the only form I could see was my own Form: Class 3C. The teacher, unaware of my lexical difficulty, and observing only a small boy who was not doing what he had been told to do, took the opportunity to give me a severe telling-off. This, I observe now, was a good example of what we might appropriately call powerlessness.

Powerlessness, essentially, is being at the mercy of others. It is something which we all experience at one time or another, and it takes many different forms. At the level of personal relations, powerlessness is the experience of 'not being seen'; when people look through us or past us. And thus it is something which we are particularly prone to experience where our expectations are highest, in the deeper relationships with those for whom we care and who care for us. Powerlessness in this context is the absence of personal recognition; though the eyes engage, they see nothing. And it is always a painful experience, for neither understanding nor recognition can be compelled, but rather belong to the sphere of grace. Like friendship itself, they are sovereign and free. And so, even in the closest relationships, a true and mature trust is built on love and mutual forgiveness.

And in the public domain, too, powerlessness surrounds us on all sides. When we are small children, and habitually in a state of powerlessness with respect to our elders, we imagine that when we are grown-up, all power will be ours. But part of growing into adulthood is the realization that we are surrounded on all sides by structures of power. The teenager going to a first job interview may experience the reality of power in one of its most evident (and perhaps bruising) forms. But the middle-aged professional applying for the most senior post in the department will encounter the same problem of power, the same painful vulnerability to the power of others to affect their own life at its core.

But if we were to stop someone on the street and ask them: Who are the truly powerless people in this world and where do they live? then we would in all probability be referred to more distant parts of the world. And it is easy for us in the democratic West to point to certain countries in the Third World where a dictator has taken power into his own hands, exploiting the people for his own political and financial gain and bulwarking his position by widespread corruption, intimidation and violence. We may well point to South Africa where the majority of citizens are deprived of all their basic political rights, and all too frequently of their right to a humane existence too. Or we may look across to Eastern Europe where so often the ordinary people are powerless in the face of the immense power of the authoritarian State. Gripping images of the truly powerless are also rarely absent from our television

31

screens. We are shown moving pictures of those who lack the barest amenities of life, and whose overwhelming poverty makes them tragically vulnerable to fluctuations in their natural environment. It is these wretched and emaciated figures who are surely the truly powerless in this world.

Yes, indeed. Savage hunger is the ultimate form of powerlessness. And yet it takes other forms of which we may not be fully aware, and which are much closer to home. There are powerless people in our own society too. Those, for instance, who are seriously disadvantaged in natural gifts and by their environment; those who are not born entrepreneurs, straining at the leash, and are neither intelligent, nor dynamic. Inevitably, natural disadvantages are further enhanced by poor-quality education, poor housing, poor employment prospects, and by being subject to a system of society and of law which appears to be decidedly tilted against them. And there are others, too, who are powerless. Not very far from where I live, there is an old nuclear reactor which is running down. The workers in the village have no other source of employment and their choice is between agreeing to another nuclear plant (which although everyone declares is 'safe', nobody wants) or facing endemic unemployment. Their powerlessness takes a different form, but it is just as real.

And we would be making a great mistake if we thought that powerlessness is confined to the 'lower classes', to those who do not inherit large sums of money and whose ancestors worked long hours in mills and down coal-mines. Powerlessness is just as much a reality for the 'under-achiever' born into a professionally high-powered and successful family. Or for the London commuter who travels for two hours to work and who has to pay off an enormous mortgage. The 'system' itself is seemingly all-powerful, and

32

it forces us, whether we work at the top or the bottom, into particular tracks and paths with which we must somehow seek to accommodate ourselves. A recent prime minister of Italy, who was a committed Christian, was asked why he did not put certain radical plans into action. He replied that if he did so, he would lose his job by the end of the week. And so, even when it might seem that we have the greatest power, we can remain in essence powerless.

Powerlessness dogs us all; it circumscribes our existence.

And we have not yet considered those minorities in modern Britain who are most likely to find themselves in a situation of powerlessness: women, whose talents often lack social recognition and who experience numerous subtle forms of economic and legal oppression; coloured people, who are constantly vulnerable to racial prejudice and disadvantage. There is our own total powerlessness as a race before the often overweening and anti-human 'life' of technology where the latter constitutes a threat to the planet itself, our life-base.

Whether we are good or bad, rich or poor, whether we are slow-witted or intelligent, beautiful, ugly or plain ordinary, powerlessness is one dimension which we have in common and which is the mark of our common humanity. And the greatest form of powerlessness of all is that which we ultimately experience with respect to our own body. There are few of us who have not, or will not, experience at some point in our lives the devastating effects of illness when our entire world seems to collapse as the physical basis for it, which we had always taken for granted, is suddenly removed. Then small, unsteady steps can become an achievement which is as great and as fought-for as any in our lives. Anyone who has seen a dying person on a hospital bed ('stranded upon the vast and lonely shore of his bleak bed', as the poet R. S. Thomas puts it), transfixed by tubes, will know what powerlessness means. 'Our little life' is indeed 'rounded with a sleep' and death through illness will prove for many of us to be the ultimate experience of our powerlessness in the face of the very forces which have guaranteed us life.

And for many, of course, the existence of so much suffering in the world seems a good reason for turning away from religious faith. It is easy enough at times to think of God as imperious and remote, an unaccountable Chairman of the Corporation whose splendid office is a thousand miles removed from the harsh reality of the factory floor. And indeed, such a God would be worthy of denial. We could with a light heart proclaim his death with Nietzsche and herald the coming of a new age of human liberation!

But God is different. The utter simplicity of truth is different.

For it is precisely in our powerlessness that God speaks to us and is present to us, and it is there above all that we can learn to discern his beauty.

What does this mean? It means something miraculous. It means that the fundamental experience which touches us at all levels of our existence, this powerlessness, is for us *a potent form of prayer and a way towards God.* For it is here that we find the Powerless One who suffered abuse, misunderstanding and finally crucifixion. In the powerless areas of our own lives the Crucified One draws near; in the bottomless, meaningless suffering which befalls all of us at one time or another, and where we are most intensely alive, Jesus, the Crucified and Powerless One, is closer to us than we are to ourselves.

We have spoken of powerlessness as a prayer, and we have spoken of Jesus. And to him, without doubt, suffering was part of his relationship with his Father; it was not something he turned away from and rejected. Jesus, the

34

'Aim That the truth!

NOW

Son of God, felt the ultimate suffering, which was the loss of the Father. In the words *Eli, Eli, lama sabach-thani?* Jesus utters all the moments of despair of all humankind, all the injured innocence, all the wounding, all the hopelessness. In his abandonment by the Father he touches the greatest depths of human suffering, contains it and takes it up within himself for all eternity. But even here, in this zero-point of existence, Jesus still says Yes to the Father.

To pray the prayer of powerlessness is in one sense the easiest prayer of all; we do not need exceptional gifts in order to know suffering, nor do we need to look long and hard in order to find it. All too often suffering seeks us out. And each time it does so we find ourselves in a place of decision. The natural temptation is to say No and to reject suffering; it is to retreat from existence, dazed and perplexed, and to allow suffering (in its most acute forms) to become a nightmare, something entirely alien which breaks in upon normality and which resists assimilation into the remainder of our existence. Then it becomes something we shall look back upon as a disjointed, utterly meaningless chapter of our lives, as a wild animal rudely parading through our carefully nurtured garden uprooting our best bushes, squashing our most delicate plants and which might (how well we know it!) at any moment return.

But there is an alternative response which is, like Jesus, simply to say Yes. This does not mean, of course, that we do not take the normal steps to relieve or avoid suffering (there can be no value in a morbid preoccupation with what is unpleasant or in an exaggerated passivity before it), but rather it is a fundamental act of assent to God whereby we say Yes to him, and not only to him but also to ourselves, to our own existence and to the world. And the way in which we say Yes is by looking for his Son in our suffering: the Powerless One who is present to us

35

wherever and whenever suffering exists. We need to love him there, where he is disfigured and hurt, marginalized and brutalized, where he is tortured and exposed defence-less to the ferocity of sin, where he is misunderstood and mocked, where he is abandoned and betrayed. We need to allow him into our lives so that he can take possession of what is rightfully his. For without him, the Powerless and Crucified One, our religious life will remain superficial, fragile and constantly exposed to upset through the vicissi-tudes of human existence. Just as a life without suffering would be wholly insipid and shallow, an inner life which does not know the crucified Jesus and does not wish to know him is one in which a fundamental (and in many ways the deepest part) of ourselves and our experience is closed off from God, held back from him. To acknowledge the Powerless One is in fact to take into our lives the most enormous source of strength and victory.

There is a beautiful meditation by a modern Italian spiritual writer, Chiara Lubich, in which she tells of know-ing Jesus in this way. She speaks of him as her 'one Spouse on earth' and says that 'in him there is the whole of para-dise with the Trinity and all the earth with mankind'. She vows to seek out her Spouse everywhere: 'What hurts me is mine. Mine the suffering that grazes me at this moment. Mine the suffering of the person next to me. Mine all that is not peace, not joy, not beautiful, not lovable, not serene. . .'. She 'will thirst for suffering, anguish, despair, separation, exile, forsakenness, torment, for all that is in him and he is Suffering'. But far from being a morbid fascination with suffering, this meditation speaks of the fearless joy which is the awesome inheritance of everyone who seeks to follow the Christian way: 'In this way . . . I shall pass as a fire that consumes everything that must die and leaves only the truth standing.'

36

Jesus, the Powerless and Forsaken One, is not an optional extra within Christianity; he is the true, liberating heart of our Christian existence. We cannot draw close to God without learning to know him. By living in him, in and through our suffering and the suffering of others, suffering wherever it might be, we will begin to live a life that is alive with his mystery: a life in which we can say, like St Paul, that 'it is no longer I who live, but Christ who lives in me' (Galatians 2:20).

Spiritual beauty is the theme we have taken for this book, spiritual beauty as the content and sign of a life lived in God. It might seem in some ways strange to use this motif when we speak of the world's suffering. And yet there is meaning in it. Spiritual beauty is not the beauty of the world; its harmoniousness is transcendent and is a thing of God. Spiritual beauty is at its greatest where we, the human dimension, are most open, willing and accepting of God's will for us, where we are most permeated by the divine. It is the place where we are broken open and the divine light is able to shine through the natural order, our ordinary lives; it is the place of blessedness, sacredness and wholeness. And so paradoxical though it might seem, the terribly disfigured face of Jesus on the cross, dying for our sins in a deep, deep Yes to the Father, spoken for all creation, is the point of greatest beauty. It is here that the human and the divine are closest and their union is brought to its greatest tension in a way that defines our own spiritual existence. This is a beauty which we too can learn, though we do so slowly in the very depths of our own being and experience. It is the strange beauty of the crucifixion in which the divine suffers the world at its deepest level, but, remaining divine, remaining utterly glorious and transcendent, it takes all the suffering and meaninglessness of

37

the world up into itself, transforming and transfiguring it in the explosion of light which is the life of the resurrection.

QUESTIONS TO ASK OURSELVES

1   Do I reject the suffering that befalls me in my life? Do I allow it to make me turn from God? Does suffering come to be a place of alienation from God in my life or does it bring me nearer to him?

2   Am I aware enough of the face of Christ in my suffering? Do I see him there? Do I trust him? Do I love him?

3   Am I aware of my own powerlessness, or do I like to pretend that I have more power than I actually have? Do I in fact console myself in my powerlessness by exercising power over others? Do I *enjoy* the sense of power I sometimes have over others?

4   How much do I allow the suffering of others to move me? Or is it easier sometimes to say that it is their own fault, that only the strong can survive, or simply to say that it is none of my business?

5   Do I see God's beauty in suffering, a beauty which is not of this world? Do I see the presence of the Powerless and Crucified One in the abject misery and meaninglessness which is sometimes our experience of this world? Can I turn suffering to spiritual joy by discovering him, my Beloved, in the midst of the world's sadness?

4

The Prayer of Poverty

To be poor in self is to be rich in God. This is a paradox which is central to Christian living. The more we insist on having our own way, proclaiming ourselves by our words and actions, the more we keep God at a distance, blocking him off with walls which are high and thick and which are built of every individual occasion when we have preferred to keep the company of ourselves and not of God, to follow our will and not his. Who is there in this world who is not burdened with an abundance of self and yet, at the same time, deep within themselves, whether consciously or unconsciously, does not feel a great hunger for that pure, clean, eternal life, that living water, which flows from only one place: the very bottom of the long, dark well-hole which is true poverty of spirit?

We live in a Me and Mine culture; our world is one which is materialistic to the core. The media, newspapers and television, which are so important a part of our daily living, urge us on all sides to discover our appetites, to possess and to desire. We are encouraged to discard what we already have and to buy the very newest, 'revolutionary' and 'new-formula' things; yesterday's washing-machine will not do. Advertising makes us feel like special guests, like kings and queens, at a consumer feast, who drive fast cars, sport the latest fashions, use the best soaps and keep the exclusive company of other best-soap users. But where does it all lead?

The answer is that it takes us nowhere. The object of desire in a world of desire is desire itself: there is no substance here but only the projection of ourselves into a vacuum: the fantasy world of fulfilment. In being encouraged to buy, we are encouraged to become somebody we are not. And what of the premises which underlie it? Surely we are being told that we *are* what we *have*. This is true materialism. And it is a false gospel, just as the perpetual stimulation of our desires fosters false and shallow forms of living. To give in to the pressure endlessly to desire and to possess is to chain ourselves to a hamster-wheel which spins round and round, taking us nowhere.

We are what we have. This is that aspect of materialism which penetrates every corner of our world (and every corner of our own soul, if we are not careful!). For instance, it is so often assumed that it is the money we earn which gives sole value to our work. Earning, possessing and being seen to possess can become so important in our culture that they threaten to swamp the more delicate and more fundamental values of personhood and self-expression. How quickly the wage-packet (or salary) can turn into a form of slave-master! Money leads us by the nose where it will, into lifestyles which are exhausting and pernicious, into jobs for which we are not suited and in which we are fundamentally unfulfilled, into ways of life and being which are at the deepest level alien to the way we truly want to live and to be. And this is not an affliction of the rich alone. The sense of self as an accumulator of goods can be as firmly rooted in those who have little as it can in those who have much.

The first thing we must do, then, if we wish to live a life of beauty in the world of today is challenge the idol of money. And there is one place above all where we can do this more effectively than in any other: within ourselves. If materialism is a particular weakness of the age of affluence and the microchip, then we will be foolish indeed if we assume that we are free of it. Rather, we can be sure that it is ready at any moment to appear in our own garden, indeed to swamp it when given the least chance. And so we must be constantly on our guard.

When we look at a painting by a great artist, we are often struck by the sense of economy there is within it. Nothing goes too far; there is nothing superfluous or out of place. In the same way there is spareness in spiritual beauty, and balance, and so a life of beauty is a life without excess. The shops are full of every kind of gadget, every kind of toy and indulgence. Now, of course it is not wrong to buy a colour television or a radio cassette recorder, but every time we feel the impulse to spend money we must submit the request to conscience, and we must be prepared to refrain if our conscience doesn't think it is such a good idea. The spending of money is a moral act, and what we do with our financial resources cannot be removed from the rest of our life in the belief, or under the pretence, that it is somehow 'private'. If we have a surplus and wish to invest it, then we cannot lend the money to firms (in our 'private' life) who do the very things we disapprove of (in our 'public' life). There is always the danger of leaving areas of our existence as a kind of well-heeled agnosticism. A life of beauty is spare and disciplined; it is an aware life in which we know the consequences of our actions and take responsibility for what we do.

But there are many forms of materialism. Take for instance those occasions when we allow undue concern for money to affect our actions. Of course, we all need to live within our means, and it is responsible and right that we

41

should do so, but still it is all too easy to allow that slave-master into our life, sometimes in the very smallest of ways. We can be penny-pinching, causing ourselves and others needless inconvenience. We can allow a natural sense of economy to become a lack of generosity, when we fail to give others in their need the benefit of the doubt. And how wonderful and releasing it is sometimes to do something for somebody else without being paid! Simply to do it because it seems the right thing to do. To do it because the doing of it is fine and fulfilling. We all need to earn a living, but then we all need to retain a sense of the precious-ness of human work as a value within itself as well. And we often need to relearn the value of making a contribution, of doing something which we can do and do well, for somebody else.

And there is another, wonderful way in which we can challenge the grotesque idol of money, which seems to stand at every street corner: that ugly, empty deity which, it is so often assumed, governs everybody's life. We can simply give money away! There is much generosity in people and a willingness to give to help others. This kind of spontaneous, explosive giving has great power, but we also need to hold before our eyes its immense *rightness*. It is a form of giving which points to the deep, spiritual truth that we are all ultimately one. My reality is your reality, and your reality is mine. And there is a further value within this act of giving, one moreover which tends to be ignored. It is a potent form of self-purification, from our sin in general, but in particular it is a strong bulwark against that deep-rooted 'modern' sin of loving things more than God. The Middle Ages knew its spiritual value well, and almsgiving was frequently recommended as a form of pen-ance in order to make up for ways in which we have abused ourselves and our fellow human beings. Giving money

42

away is indeed a potent act and, in the kind of society in which we live, it is perhaps more revolutionary, more dangerous and more evangelically subversive than any other!

Materialism indeed takes many forms, but its root is always the same: possessiveness. We are materialistic when we say to God: This is mine and not yours. And one place in which we are inclined to do that more than any other is in our own bodies. After all, what is more natural than that we should feel that the body we inhabit, the body we *are*, is ours to do what we want with. It is our toy, our reality, our temple to do what we like with . . . There are many little ways in which we abuse our bodies, seeking stimulation, and making it pay for what is wrong in our lives or in us. We might find that sometimes we eat too much, or eat the wrong kind of food (a diet which may seem familiar and congenial enough but which we know will do damage to our body in the long run). We may find that we drink too much alcohol, that we smoke. There are many ways, sometimes gross and sometimes subtle, in which we say to God: This is my body and I'll do what I like with it. And the area of our life in which this is the greatest threat, of course, is our own sexuality.

There exists at the very root of our sexual being a tension between our desire to possess and our desire to share. Indeed, this is a tension that underlies all our moral being: a conflict between the drive to exploit and control others and the wisdom that allows them to be as they are. But it is a tension which is most visible in our sexual life. So often the imagery of modern living, the world of media and advertising which surrounds us all, prompts in us the desire for exploitation: the exploitation of women by men and of men by women. How deeply sexuality is drawn into that false and glossy consumer world of fast cars and beautiful bodies; the female (and male) form appears to be an article of consumption among all the others. It is there to titillate our desires and to convince us that we belong to this hard-sheen world of instant desire. And yet, underlying this superficially attractive world is a deep human disorder. It is the dislocation of the whole person by the removal of sexuality from its authentic place at the heart of relationship. Of course, there is fun in sexual attraction, and there is all the intoxicating excitement of courtship. But sexuality leads towards the human person and not away. It is a statement of love and commitment and of the attraction between the sexes which extends to all levels of our existence. And thus the proper place for a full sexuality is marriage. This is so not on account of a prudish fear of the language of the body, or of a kill-joy desire to restrict it; but because of the true nature of sexuality itself, which feeds and grows rich upon a diet of committed love and mutual sharing which takes in the whole of our living and which finds its fullest expression in the context of married life. It is this alone which provides a truly adequate context in which sexuality can flourish and can fully be the great gift which it is.

But one thing is certain: for someone (especially a young person) to live a life of sexual purity today requires the courage to go against the stream. It requires the willingness to love God and to accept his law in our lives. It requires the determination to be the person God wants us to be. For all the pressures in our society are materialistic, and materialism in sexuality begins when we divorce the sexual language of the body from the emotional life of sustaining love, which is its sole true context. And there is a danger that we have forgotten the generative dimension of sexuality with its attendant responsibilities and commitments. We have put it on the shop shelf for all to see and all to covet. And so this most primal, personal and beautiful life of the body and the senses, which is a sacred sphere suffused with warm companionship and love, can seem an alien, celluloid and impersonal object, stolen from us, its true possessors, and exhibited in the neon-lit heart of a throw-away world.

Spiritual poverty takes many forms but it is in essence that God-given moment when we say Yes to what is good, wholesome and right and No to what is evil. It is not a permanent state; rather, it is a point in time, a moment of transition from one way of living to another. It is the moment when we say Yes to life itself in all its uplifting vigour and No to the dull mediocrity which is the world of self-interest.

We call this moment poverty, for it occurs when we choose God's way and take leave of our own. And nowhere will we find a higher example of what we mean here than when Jesus said: 'Thy will be done.' That was the moment of poverty when the human nature of Christ bowed to the divine nature. It was a point at which Jesus said Yes to the will of the Father, allowing there to come upon him all kinds of suffering. A king, he was condemned a criminal; a peacemaker, he was executed for stirring up sedition; God's precious Son, he was mocked and pilloried and torn apart 'by dogs'. We can call this kind of poverty humility, or self-emptying, and there are many different ways in which it can enter our life. Take those areas in which we are not free, for instance; the need to smoke, perhaps, or the need to 'have a go' at people behind their backs. That too is a form of compulsion. Or the need to look at women in the wrong way, seeing only their sexuality and not the wholeness of their being. Or the tendency to pettiness, jealousy or vanity. Each time we refrain from these 'little'

45

things, we create a space within ourselves which can be filled with God. And we must savour him as he takes up residence in us afresh, each time we deny ourselves and say Yes to his reality above ours.

And then there is another, very common way in which we learn that poverty of spirit which we call humility. This is when something happens, someone says something, which seems to steal from us what feels to be rightfully ours: our dignity. Those are moments when something in us rebels, long and loudly, and when we are confronted with a choice of whether to submit passively or to 'kick up a fuss'. There are a thousand such occasions in our lives when we feel our true worth has not been recognized. These are moments when we may feel: does this person not know who I am? Do they not see how nice I am being when I could really be quite nasty? Do they not see how clever I am? Or perhaps someone has been rude to us without provocation, on the street, on a bus, in our work, while shopping. It is easy to get indignant then, to make a mental note to get one's own back, to throw them a black look, to protest. But this is not the way of the cross: the way of spiritual poverty. It is to say Me and Mine, when we should acknowledge that God is leading us by the hand along a path which perhaps for the moment is dark and uncongenial. He is testing us to see whether we love him, he is prodding us where we are flabby, he is teaching us to shed barren notions about ourselves which contain and restrict truer and deeper forms of being. And, as such, these occasions are to be welcomed: the many little injuries to pride, the slights intentional and unintentional, the mis-understandings of what we mean and assumptions of what we don't mean ('Do they really think I could say something so stupid?'). These are opportunities for us to say Yes to God, to lose a little of that spiritual 'flab'. And the loss of

46

a flabby ego is a great blessing; it is a release and a liberation from a whole network of defensive–aggressive responses, which are founded in no little degree on our own insecurity, and which cause us quite as much discomfort as they do everyone else.

Humility, which is true poverty of spirit, is the jewel in the crown of the life of beauty. It often has the hardest lessons to teach us, but its wisdom is the most liberating. How absurd it is that we should spend so much time and energy in defence of what is ultimately alien to us: that false illusion of self-importance, the pomposity of self-love. Sometimes we seem like those crusader knights of old who, in great cumbersome suits of armour, would drag their limbs onto the battlefield in the heat of the mid-day sun. Far better to leave it all at home!

God's goodness is abundant. God has given us existence itself: that banquet of delight at which we are favoured guests. God has given us all good gifts: this world with its beauty that can astonish, the innumerable forms of natural life with their breathtaking intricacy, all the convolutions of a material world which sustains, contains and supports us. God holds us in the palm of her hand with all the care and tenderness of a mother. And yet, however great this generosity, the wealth and abundance of God's giving, we can and do reject God's goodness to us. And this happens, paradoxically, when we forget who it is that gives us these things. Our instinct is to take, and not to receive. We learn to demand, and forget how to ask.

In the age to which we belong, a life based on loving poverty is a radical challenge; it is a revolution. To love poverty in all its forms, as humility, as purity of spirit, as material moderation, as self-discipline, is to acknowledge God as the source of all being and to honour the hand of God as that which sustains and supports us. Only in this

47

way can we receive the unutterable goodness of God to us. To be poor in God is to put God's will before our own; it is to lay down our sense of self as that which demands and possesses and desires. It is to learn how to ask and to receive. It is, in the truest sense, to become a child of God so that she may be to us a loving Mother.

And yet poverty can be more even than this. It can be the loss of self for the sake of the God who is More. It was Meister Eckhart who said: 'As far as you depart from all things, thus far, no less and no more, does God enter into you, with all that is his.' But it is a wealth that is not of this world: it is a living stream of life, a fragrance and a delight, a sense of liberty and space. It is a moment of hope and of vision when, through the accepting of God's will rather than our own, heaven enters into us, light shines through us, and we are made luminous and whole. And so poverty above all, the poverty which comes from God, is a place of abundance.

QUESTIONS TO ASK OURSELVES

1 Do I spend a disproportionate amount on myself and my own needs? Is there anywhere where I can cut down in a way that would improve my life as a whole?

2 Am I a slave to money in any way? Do I allow it to determine excessively what I do and what I don't do?

3 Do I give enough money away to charity? Or only an amount which is so low that it scarcely matters?

4 Do I abuse my body, feeling that I have the right to do with it what I will? Are there areas of physical abuse from which I banish God and conscience?

5   Do I struggle to keep myself sexually pure (either inside or outside marriage)? Do I accept the discipline of poverty in this area, which is purity?

6   Do I carry around a 'flabby' ego? When I feel insulted or slighted, can I transform my response into a love of poverty, which is humility?

7   Do I thank God every day for the joy and the fullness of existence?

5

The Prayer of Love

And so we come to love which, magnificent and explosive, is the radiance at the heart of a life of beauty. The nature of God himself is love; and it is when we love that we are closest to him. It is when we love that we become a window for his light, or an open space in an area of darkness where God's light can fall.

But love is not just light; it is energy too. Love seeks incarnation; it strives to become flesh among us. It is not the nature of love to remain light, like a sky high above us; it wants also to be rain, which falls to earth to fertilize the ground and, finally, it wants to become root, set fast in the deep earth. But as sky and rain and root, love remains life.

This is the miracle of love, that it should be rooted simultaneously in heaven and earth, and that it should be the meeting place of what is incomplete, faltering and of this world with what is true, powerful, eternal and divine. This is why love is life for us; it is the light and energy by which we live. And it is the reason too why love is a mystery to us, for Christian love is God's touching of the soul. It is the fire of the Spirit which remains beyond our understanding. This love, which is God's gift and which is neither us nor him but both, transforms us from within. It challenges us; it breaks down the old mechanical behaviour of the person we have been and gives strength to the truer and more real person we become. Love cleanses us and purifies us, stripping from us all that is dark and half-hearted, all that is dull and unclean. And it lends to our nature, with all its faults, something which is of God.

And so love is spirit and it is fire, but it is incarnation too, in the most ordinary areas of our living. It is simple concern for others, humane toleration of the weak and compassion for those who suffer. A disembodied love, floating around in our minds, is neither one thing nor the other. Love forces incarnation; it wills to become flesh in the very centre of our lives.

And we do not need to journey far in order to find where love is born. It is not a remote place nor is it difficult to find. In fact, the path of love begins in the most everyday of places: our neighbour. The person next to us, wherever we happen to be, is the doorway to love for us. And that is where the problems begin!

People make demands. Take our families, for instance, which present a whole world of potential problems and mutual responsibilities. We can get very used to thinking of our families as moving pieces of furniture which, every once in a while, get in the way. It often takes an act of will to love the people we know best, wholeheartedly. Instead of scoring points off each other, instead of avoiding domestic chores that need to be done, instead of taking out our own fluctuating moods upon others in the family, we need to make a special effort of love, so that our family life can be constantly renewed by the energy of the Spirit and of love. What seems too familiar to us can easily be abused. What is wonderful, miraculous even and of the deepest significance for our lives can easily be taken for granted and misunderstood.

And then there are the people we do not like: those who offend us or irritate us in some way. Sometimes such antipathy can be quite natural and is the result of the way that others choose to behave. But sometimes it can be quite irrational, when we may feel an impulsive, unaccountable dislike of somebody else. Most generally, though, such antipathy is the result of seeing our own personal faults in others. If we are impractical and inclined to shy away from the needful realities of life, then this inclination in others can get under our skin. If we are vain, the vanity of others stretches our nerves. If we are dominating, we dislike others who dominate. People we do not like make demands. But we must always ask ourselves in all honesty what it is about them that causes this response in us. If it is their uncivilized behaviour, then it is worth reminding ourselves that brutal people have inevitably themselves been brutalized. This does not necessarily solve the immediate problem, but it does add the consoling light of understanding. Human relations are a chain reaction and we must take great care that we do not allow ourselves to become yet another link in that chain. If someone treats us unfairly, then we must watch that we don't treat them, or anyone else, unfairly too. If we become the victim of unkindness or even brutality of some kind, then we must not make others the victim of our own unkindness. Someone must call a halt to the 'tit for tat'. That chain must be broken. This is the meaning of Jesus' words when he tells us to turn the other cheek (Luke 6:29). It is only through the courageous preparedness to accept suffering without hitting back that peace may return to where violence reigns and the cycles of brutality can be broken. Finally, of course, we may find that our antipathy to others is founded upon no more than our own pettiness or prejudice. In this case we must make a great effort to love such people with a special love and to destroy that within us which despises others for simply being the person they are.

It was Jean-Paul Sartre who said: 'Hell is other people.' And, indeed, there may be moments in the company of difficult people when we might be inclined to agree! But other people are heaven too: 'Behold, how good and pleasant it is when brothers dwell in unity!' (Psalm 133:1). When love is shared, when peace is restored, when there is mutual trust and respect, when we are prepared to suffer for the sake of love and for the other person, then Jesus himself is present among us. That is a very special delight – when we feel him among us as a fragrant, sustaining and sanctifying presence. There is so much in us which is centred on the self. Other people can so easily seem a threat to our own interests, peace of mind or even spirituality. But something in us is incomplete until we have felt and known for ourselves the sense of Jesus among us. Something in us is being denied until we have known him in this – communal – way as his Church and his people in a communion and a sharing of love.

Love begins wherever we are: in the here and now. And so each context for love is different: it may be the struggle to refresh and renew a relationship with our marriage partner or our children within the cycle of daily living (the same problems, the same responses . . .), or it may be the attempt to greet as a friend somebody we have never met before. And yet, in all the bewildering variety of human life, love remains the same. It is the preparedness to accept and affirm the 'other' precisely in their otherness, to take the first step. It is a readiness to live in the present moment, and to forget all the accumulated grievances and injuries which, like tenacious weeds, threaten the new growth in a relationship. But above all, it is the readiness to leave behind the person we have been and to welcome the new person we must become: that self who is God's own creation, wrought by God through our striving, our saying

53

Yes, in all the tangle and difficulty of our daily living. God, in this respect, is a potter who works with human clay. He is a sculptor who works with the human form, and each cut of his chisel is a moment when we accept him within the ever-changing reality of our relations with other people.

And yet it might seem that to speak of love in this way is to make it sound easy. But love is not easy: that is something which every human being knows, whatever their age and circumstances. Sometimes loving is the hardest and most challenging thing we can do. For to love is in a way to die; it demands crucifixion. When we allow 'space' to someone else to be themselves in all their otherness, then we must allow ourselves to be transformed: to become light and energy, to be transparent. And this transparency is both the most effortless and the most demanding thing we can achieve. It involves saying Yes with our very being, to God and to the other person, even when they do things which we do not like; when they are destructive, blinkered and ignorant. When they assault us and seek to destroy us, whether in large dramatic ways, or in ways that are small and private and scarcely noticeable to others. To love is in essence to be prepared to suffer for the sake of somebody else, and somebody, perhaps, we do not know or do not like. Clearly, to this extent love seems impossible – to us anyway. It challenges us to act beyond our powers: more like angels than ordinary, flesh-and-blood human beings. Love of this type, we may feel, true and heroic love, is for the saints.

And yet all love is true and is heroic. And all love takes us beyond our own powers and, potentially at least, into areas of ourselves, capacities, which we never knew existed. For all love, ultimately, is gift: the gift of God who is himself love. That is why the call to love God comes first, before the commandment to love our neighbour as ourselves. For loving our neighbour depends upon our saying Yes to God, as he moves in us as primal love. It is by his power that we can love those who hate us, and rise above all those natural instincts which would lead us to return hatred with hatred and violence with violence. This is a miracle of Christian living which can only happen when the loving God himself takes residence in us; when we become a fortress of his love, a channel for the great love God has, which thrusts itself through us into the world. When he makes us truly his children.

Love, then, is a serious business; it touches the very heart of things. It is the measure of our preparedness to follow Christ; to walk with him on his long road to Calvary. We are always tempted to set limits and to defend ourselves, while love calls us to follow Christ in his vulnerability and transforming exposure to the world. We are tempted to regard others as a threat, to block them off and to control them; to set limits on our involvement with people. And yet this is not the way of Christ. He leads us towards others and towards the world. He tells us to accept others (in their 'otherness'), and to turn the other cheek (if need be). His message is one of involvement and vulnerability, of contact and concern. Above all, it is a message of unity and of making ourselves one with others. We cannot withdraw into our citadel of defences, and still follow Christ in this intimate area of human relations. We cannot 'write people off' and regard them as alien objects to whom we have no absolute relation. The call to discipleship here is precisely a call to a readiness to suffer for the sake of others, even (and especially) when they are awkward and cantankerous, blinkered and unaccommodating. For still, like us, they are made in God's image, and like us are infinitely precious to God.

The Christian message of love is one that turns the world

on its head. The unwritten principle which underlies our social relations is generally one of enlightened self-interest: 'As long as you leave me in peace, I'll leave you in peace, but if you do step out of line, then I'll stop being your friend and I'll become your enemy. And then you'll really have to watch out.' But is that enough? Is that what Christ meant when he said: 'May they all be one' (John 17:23)? When he said: 'Love your neighbour as yourself' (Matthew 19:19)? Or is this kind of love, the 'new commandment', something deeper?

Of course it is! And a Christianity which fails to understand this cannot be a discipleship following that same Lord. If we want to follow him, if we want to claim Christ and for him to claim us, then we must live a love that is radical, that goes to the root of things. We must make ourselves vulnerable, as Christ made himself vulnerable for us. We must learn the long and difficult lesson of dying to ourselves so that Christ may live, who is love. We must make ourselves empty before him, accepting the pain and marginalization which may come. And, if we do this, slowly but surely something in us will change. Like John the Baptist, we will diminish and Christ will increase (John 3:30). We will become new. We will no longer be alien to God, nor he to us. But rather, we will become the friend of God, we shall walk with him. He will be our lover and our spouse.

And just think where we could begin! How many thousands of opportunities to love have we had already, and how many have we squandered? Each encounter with another person is an opportunity to choose Heaven. Each and every time we sense within ourselves a closing-off from other people (people we do not like; in whose company we feel awkward; people with certain mannerisms that annoy us; people with attitudes which make us see red). There is no interaction, however slight, which cannot be illumined by love. This is a radical revolution of love, when everyone becomes for us an opportunity to witness to Christ, to tell him privately in the depths of our heart that we choose him and his way of light. We cannot love unless we become like him, vulnerable and alive, fully part of the world and of the heavenly order. We should indeed give thanks for each and every opportunity to choose God in this way.

And there are in every society those who prompt our 'choice of love' in a very special way. There are those persons who challenge us in that they somehow embody physical, mental or psychological weakness: forms of weakness, that is, which perhaps ultimately remind us of our own fragility. How easy it is to ignore such people, perhaps in the subtlest of ways. I well remember an occasion when I was teaching a class among whom there was one intelligent handicapped man who had difficulty in speaking clearly. While aware of his presence, and full of goodwill towards him, I didn't address any questions directly to him. And I didn't do so, I realized later, because of my own feeling of – potential – embarrassment. Thus in a subtle way I was rejecting his handicap and, of course, Paul the person with it. If I put a question to Paul, the person I was seeing but keeping at a distance, then I would have accepted his handicap and I would have accepted him. And I am sure that I, and perhaps he too, would have been richer for it.

There are precious people therefore who act as catalysts for our love. People who have some disability which disconcerts us by reminding us of our own many weaknesses and forms of frailty. And it need not be the physically handicapped, it can also be those who are socially handicapped. People who wear the right hat on the wrong occasion, those who have not quite mastered the 'right' kind of vocabulary for the situation: the weak, the gauche, the misfits. And ultimately the truth is perhaps that we are all 'weak, gauche and misfits', only some of us conceal our weaknesses more effectively than others. And so in loving those special people, we are at the same time loving and accepting ourselves in our own fragility and weakness.

Everywhere in the religious world today new and old forms of spirituality are emerging. This is something which extends far beyond the borders of the Christian churches even; it is a response which seems to be deeply rooted within many people who do not necessarily find what they are seeking in the Christian life. Now certainly this call for what is spiritually *real* is a right and proper thing, and it is something which corresponds to what is a deep change within our culture. We are no longer content to accept religion on anybody else's word; we need to know for ourselves. We need to experience. Christianity, no longer an ideology (in our culture at least), has to appeal to the whole person within the context of our contemporary living. But this development brings with it a danger: the risk that something all-important may be forgotten: our neighbour. Jesus told us that one of the highest commandments of the law was to love God with all our hearts and minds and bodies, and these words of his are surely the foundation for all spirituality. And yet at the same time he added that we are to love our neighbour as ourselves. How often has the second proposition been forgotten in the history of Christianity, and how often has spirituality become something lame and, in a sense, hollow precisely because it lacked the outreach, the overflow, the abundance of life which is embodied in our love for our neighbour?

Even spirituality can become a self-centred thing. It can become a way of blocking others off, of defending ourselves against a cold and unsympathetic world. And yet, if God is love, and our spirituality is the love we have for him who is love, then it cannot be a retreat. It can only be an advance: an advance into life, and into that reality which is our neighbour. And it can only be a loving advance, in which we put aside what is ours in favour of what is theirs. Our spirituality must be a movement then towards our neighbour, which is a movement into vulnerability, and living concern.

Love is a call to a new life; it is a transforming mystery. For it is when we love that we are closest to God, and most in his image. The ecstatic, free, self-giving and infinitely fertile nature of God is incarnate in our own true loving, which is always free, always concerned with what is beyond itself, always heartwarming and beautiful. And so love, rooted and incarnated in our own concrete reality, takes us beyond ourselves, into new and dynamic realities in which it is no longer we who live but Christ who lives in us. And yet love, however mysterious and however exalted, always remains in one sense the most ordinary of things. For love is a love between people; it is a saying Yes to the God of love as he comes to meet us in the most ordinary, everyday situations. And so love can become the element in which we live, and which penetrates to every dimension and depth of our lives. It can be a transforming reality, a purifying fire, a vital energy and spirit, and it can be for us ultimately a path which leads into the heart of life and into joy without end.

QUESTIONS TO ASK OURSELVES

1 Do I profess that I love God, while ignoring the needs of my neighbour? Is there a chasm between what I believe and what I do?

2   Am I loving only towards the people I like?

3   When did I last say Yes to love and allow myself to be raised beyond myself into new possibilities of being?

4   Do I live a life that is radically open and loving towards others?

5   Do I hit back at people who hurt me? Or am I prepared to accept suffering so that the cycles of sin can be broken and peace restored?

6   Am I aware enough of those times when other people show love towards me? And do I give thanks for such times?

7   Am I loving towards Christians of other denominations? Or do I prefer to wage a 'holy war' against them?

8   Am I aware of the presence of Jesus among his people? Do I seek him out and love him there?

9   Do I know God as the Fire and Spirit of love?

6

The Prayer of Delight

God is our infinite delight. God is the source of our greatest and purest joy. God dissolves us and creates us again from within. God touches us and draws us beyond ourselves into an ecstasy of love and infinite possibility. For God is the utterly beautiful.

God is the utterly beautiful. This is the very core of our Christian experience and yet, strangely, this sense of our delight in God is often absent from the formal side of religion. We Christians can sometimes seem to be excessively burdened with conscience and with a sense of what is forbidden, and our religion can seem mediocre and pedestrian; more a habit than a vocation. Yet in truth we are God's lovers and our life in him is a spring of inexhaustible delight. God too is sometimes portrayed as something quite different from what he is in truth, as something ugly. There are times when we might think of him in our own hearts as being pernicious, autocratic, small-minded and punishing. Or we may feel that God is shadowy and life-denying. These are moments when we do him great injury, like a human lover whose love we squander, manipulate or take for granted. These are the times when we lose sight of the loveliness of God and, in losing the sense of his beauty, we lose the sense of our own.

It may be that we are not accustomed to think of God as absolute beauty. We are, as a culture, peculiarly concerned with action and with purposes and ends. There is little space left in our lives for the stillness of being. And to come to understand God as beauty requires stillness: stillness and depth. It means discovering our own mystery; learning our own depth. For only what is deep can love. Shallowness has no time for anything but itself. It flows from one point of distraction to the next, never aware, never taking command of itself, or discovering direction.

And so once again, seeing the beauty of God is a reciprocal thing. We can only see him in so far as we are like him, and we can only become like him by being permeated with his beauty and his grace. As St Augustine says, he desires us for the beauty with which he himself clothes us.

The beauty of God is like a spell that falls over the whole of our life. It is a fragrance that passes everywhere. Seeing this beauty is like falling in love. And just as when we have a human lover, this seeing the beauty of God, this falling head over heels in love with God, is something that changes us at all levels of our being. We are never the same again. It teaches us to look at everything in a new way. And this is not something which happens only once and then is past. Rather, this love experience grows and deepens, changing with the years: just as the feelings of an old husband and wife are not those they shared on their wedding day, and yet in a sense are still the same, so too we grow in our love for God, always changing and deepening, always discovering new depths of light in him and, by that light, new depths in ourselves.

Nothing in life ever remains still; this is as true of our love as it is of anything else. All is subject to change, and what is not nurtured will die. So the love we have for another person needs constantly to be fuelled by little acts of kindness, an acknowledgement of their specialness and their otherness. These acts may be small enough (doing

62

the washing-up; making the tea; not getting cross when we generally do!) but they express our awareness of a relationship of love and our desire to allow it to grow and to be. These acts of love strengthen the relationship and keep it healthy, so when there is a challenge we are best able to cope with it.

It is the same with our life in God. For though there is nothing more powerful than the things of the spirit, nothing is more easily pushed aside or forgotten. If we do not nurture our relationship with God, then, like everything else, it will wither away. And the way in which we can best do this is by bringing him to mind in the little everyday things of life. We can set time aside to pray each day, for instance, or if we find that we have to do something unwelcome or unpleasant, then through an inner act of intention we can carry it out for him. If we see an opportunity to help someone, then we can help them as an act for him. And if we experience misfortune, or are misjudged in some way, then we can offer our suffering to him. We can try, in other words, to bring all aspects of our existence into his presence. In this way we will find that we have a sense of walking with God, in truth of being and truth of living.

But learning to see God's beauty can be one of the most difficult things of all to do and is the lesson of a lifetime. Discovering his ravishing form in all the humdrum shapes and images of our daily living, discovering him, his transfigured and transfiguring glory, in all the partialness, the unsatisfactoriness, the tawdriness of our existence, discovering our love for him which is above all other loves – this is the long life-work of the Christian lover. And yet, in another way, it is the easiest thing of all. For our love for God is an answer to the love he bears us, and our desire for him is created by his desire for us. The truth and loveliness of God seek us out in the ground of our being. And yet how often we are tempted to see him as something he is not – to reduce him, to make him fit into our ordinary world. We seem in all manner of ways to wish to constrain him, to force him to be something which we can understand in our own terms. The truth is that with God, the discipline of love is the same discipline we find in all places: the preparedness to allow the other to be, which in this case is to allow God to be what he is: the utterly beautiful.

The idea of God's beauty, and its meaning for us in our everyday living, is an infinitely rich reality which is not always easily grasped. But we may compare it in a way to the beauty of a great work of art. And when we stand before a timeless painting, we find that we are drawn into a world of stillness. We are made to look intently, to open ourselves up to a reality beyond ourselves. We do not ask questions such as 'What is it for?' but we accept the painting as it is, for itself alone. And the joy and delight which we feel in great art stems from the very fact that it is a free expression of itself; it is a self-giving to which we can only respond in ever greater receptivity of stillness and depth. Art liberates us from the smallness and fussiness of our own too complex reality. Beauty is the communication of freedom.

If this is true of a work of art, then how much truer is it of the transcendent and living beauty of God? The sense of God's beauty summons us to stillness and to the letting go of perpetual action. It liberates us from the need always to serve some further end. It breaks the chains of functionalism, which determine so much of our daily existence. And so when we know God as the truly beautiful, we know him as one who exists for himself alone, sovereign and free. And being himself Freedom and Grace, he summons us to be what we ourselves most truly are in him: free, graceful and beautiful.

We have compared the beauty of God to that of a work of art. But let us compare his beauty also to that of a human lover. For everyone who has ever loved knows the power of the spell which beauty casts and which seems to take possession of the whole of our being. But this is a transforming passion, for it is founded most essentially upon our encounter with another person who constitutes for us another reality. Every lover knows that this discovery of the otherness of the beloved, and the desire to allow the other person to *be*, modifies, develops, and changes us in the essence of our being. This deepening sense of the other calls for an attitude of attentiveness, the awareness of another presence, where previously we went our own way. We are moulded and enriched by our beloved in a thousand different ways. Through the shared experience of living, we grow one towards the other. This, then, is the parallel for what takes place in us when we come under the spell of God's beauty. That beauty becomes a new reality for us into which we grow and in which we are transfigured. It becomes for us a new form of life.

But there is one further thing which happens then, when we allow God to woo us in this way. There is the discovery of delight. After all, this is the dominant experience we have with a human lover: the simple spontaneous delight in the being of another person, a shared being-together of mutual delight. And how true this can be of our love-affair with God, when we allow him to be what he wishes to be for us: our spiritual lover and spouse, the beginning and the end of all our desires and affections, an inner place of mystery and union.

But this love-affair with God, when we know him in the heart's image, in the ground and centre of our being, is not something which excludes the body. In fact, we are never further from God than when we run round in spiritual circles, pretending that we have no body. It is then that we need to remember that God took on a body, for us. Our bodies must be drawn into the central place of our relationship with God. We need to learn to worship him with our bodies, to adore him in and through our bodily life. This is something we can do in our prayer, by allowing our body to express an attitude of devotion; or even through forms of yoga or dance, which make the body the medium of our worship. But we can pray with our senses too. This also is a great paradox of the mystical life. We can learn to embrace God with the senses, who is beyond all sensory life. We can hold him who cannot be held; touch him, who cannot be touched; move in him, who has no dimensions; love him who is beyond all being and yet is the source of being: who is and who is not.

Our love relationship with God is fraught with paradox. And indeed how could it be otherwise? Nowhere is this sense of paradox more evident than in the use of sexual imagery to express our feelings towards God. And yet there is an ancient tradition in the Church of doing precisely this. It has good reason. After all, all lovers know that the deepest union we may have with another person is the relationship of marriage. And in this relationship sexual union is a vital part. It is not something incidental, which has become attached as it were to the rest of marriage, but is the very heart of what is a total living-together at the level of spirit, soul and body. The sexual self-giving of two lovers is at the same time their self-giving at all levels of their lives. It is complete mutual commitment. And, moreover, it is a relationship which is in the truest sense responsive and ecstatic. At the height of sexual passion, we go beyond ourselves through our love for another. We are

66

taken beyond ourselves by the potency of love, that love which is itself an echo of the divine, self-giving love which is the foundation of all things. And so human love, which is itself at its core a mystery, becomes a fit symbol for the greater mystery, which is the communion of the soul with God: a communion of love and fellowship which involves us in the entirety of our being and which draws us to a point of transcendence in which we give way to what is beyond and above the limits of our own being.

But what does it mean to have God as our Lover? In what way does our life change? The answer is simple: in all ways. Just as there can scarcely be any area of our lives which is unaffected by meeting and marrying the person we love, so too in our relationship with God there is an encounter which leaves nothing untouched. Of course, it does not all happen at once (any more than it does with a human lover), for the growing into God which is the foundation of our life in him is something which takes many years, indeed, the whole of our lives to work out. There are, above all, areas of resistance in which we are habitually unresponsive to his beauty, when we say No to him. These are the places of our own self-indulgence, our own wilfulness in which we prefer our own way to his. Such points in our existence exclude God; they wound him and ourselves. But these deep-seated areas take a long time to overcome, and the surest way of overcoming them in the end is by the *positive will to please God in all things*. This is to follow the path of what St Paul calls *areskeia* (Colossians 1:10). This Greek word means 'to want to please' and St Paul uses it to refer to our own desire to 'please' God, as we would a human lover. We love God and we delight in him: he is the object and the fullness of our desire. When we reject him, therefore, we do so in ignorance of this truth, and this blindness can best be overcome not by negative, disciplinary measures but by discovering in these areas of difficulty God's desire for us, and our own loving desire to possess God in all things, to possess him utterly and to be wholly possessed by him. The desire of and for God banishes all that is lukewarm and uncommitted in our lives and leads to true repentance – to saying sorry. It heals all that is turned away from God and is bogged down within the self. It restores a sense of life and purpose and sentience in those areas in which we habitually sin and cut ourselves off from him.

Desire for God is the life of the spirit. When we desire him, then we are alive in him. We are warm with spiritual life. And so we should desire God hugely. We should 'lust' after him with all the powers of our being. We should seek him everywhere, to possess him, to possess all that is his, to submerge ourselves in him and to surround ourselves inside and out with his living, vibrant and divine reality.

And there is one special place where God offers himself to us in his glory: the Church's liturgy. Of course, not all churches and not all church services reveal God to us to the same degree! Indeed, some services may leave us heavy with disappointment and with the sense of lost opportunity. And yet, nevertheless, Christian liturgy always and everywhere contains the transcendent beauty of God as a seed at its core which can at any moment erupt into divine splendour. This remains true whether the service concerned is one which makes use of incense and plain-chant and ancient buildings, or whether it is the barest of services in a draughty church hall. The truth is that the beauty of sound is a natural beauty and not the beauty of God at all. Its special place in liturgy is that it can, through the action of the Holy Spirit, become a sign to us of the beauty of God. It can become a doorway as it were through which God in his radiance enters our mind and heart. However frequently this may happen, this is always a most special moment when God touches us in our very being. But what of those occasions when he doesn't? – when the liturgy seems a jumble of words, and the service an automatic ritual which means nothing? Then we need to wait on God, and pray to him that he will clean away from our chalice the layers of grime and neglect and show us again the gold of which it is made.

And the sacraments are in general a golden way of entering into the life of God. Through the active presence of the Church in this way, whole areas of our lives can be taken up and made transparent to the beauty of God. The burden is removed from our own shoulders. All we need to do is to assent to the particular way in which God is acting on our behalf, whether in the Eucharist or in the service of marriage or in the sacrament of reconciliation, or in any of the other sacramental practices of the Church. Each sacrament is an opportunity to receive Christ in a new way. It is a self-offering of Christ to us in the midst of our individual lives. And by this means, by accepting and welcoming the sacraments into our lives on a regular basis, we can allow the beauty of his presence to penetrate us, to take root in us and eventually to transform us from within.

We can see God in many different ways: as King, Judge, Creator or Ruler. And yet none of these will ultimately make sense if we do not know him also as our Lover: he who is the object and the fulfilment of our truest and deepest desire. We are by our very nature creatures of desire, and ravishment is at the heart of our being. But all too often we desire what is wrong, and that which is the true object of our hunger we ignore. And so in loving God for his beauty, and being loved by him, we are restored to our own true being. In desiring him, and being desired by him, we are recreated in his beauty.

QUESTIONS TO ASK OURSELVES

1 Do I seek God in the liturgy?

2 Do I always try to be faithful to God, who is my Lover, or only intermittently so?

3 Do I allow myself times of prayer in which stillness can gather and deepen as I reflect on God's beauty?

4 Do I delight in God with the whole of my being?

5 Am I aware of how much God desires me?

6 Am I sufficiently aware of the need for repentance, and do I understand it to be the healing of a wound between lovers?

7 Have I discovered the beauty of sacraments for my life?

7

The Prayer of Transfiguration

Change is at the very centre of our being. Nothing, either within ourselves or within the world we inhabit, is permanent. All is subject to change; all is in flux. And this is true even where things most seem fixed: in the physical universe. What appears firm and solid is in reality dynamic and full of movement. The solid walls we see are millions of vibrating electrons moving at the highest speeds. The firm resistant surface we can touch is the creation of a welter of dynamic energy and movement. Even the stars which seem so timelessly still are themselves objects which are in movement at unimaginable speeds. And yet, with all this whirling, dancing movement around us, all this sparkling energy, it sometimes seems to us that one thing alone in all the universe is hopelessly stuck, bereft of energy and condemned to a circular and stagnant being: we ourselves.

We all know the experience of being caught in the rut of our own existence: the repetition of our daily chores, the tedium of self-awareness, the banality of ingrained and seemingly inescapable responses. All these serve to make us feel at times that we are going nowhere. Where we need energy, there is torpor, and where we need abundance of life, there is frustration and stagnation.

Undoubtedly episodes of this kind are simply part of our existence, part of the experience of being human, which we

71

can only accept in the reality of the present moment, while awaiting a turn for the better. And yet there are far more dangerous ways of stagnating. These are those forms of being which stem from our own wilfulness and resistance to change: the refusal to *become*. The life in God presents us at every stage with a challenge: the challenge to accept newness of being in him and newness of life. We are creatures in perpetual movement and in us nothing is fixed. Everything in us is constantly in flux and it either grows and develops or it fades and withers away. The range of options for our growth seems infinite: yet ultimately we choose in each moment of our living to grow either upwards into ever greater life and depth of being, or downwards into the shallowness and smallness of a life lived half-heartedly and with banal self-reference.

One of the areas in which we can be most resistant to growth and to change is that of our opinions. We all like to be right, at least most of the time, and yet we are constantly challenged in what we believe. How comforting it is to feel that we have arrived at the truth about something and that we need listen no longer to what anyone else has to say on the matter! And this can easily lead to something more pernicious, that tendency which afflicts us all simply to dismiss whole areas of humanity (inevitably those people with whom we feel we have least in common). We see this kind of dynamic at work in some men, for instance, who feel in their heart of hearts that women are congenitally irrational and untrustworthy creatures. We see it at work between ethnic groups, with the deep suspicion different races harbour against each other. This tendency is also sometimes painfully evident among religious groups: Catholics and Protestants, for instance, who may feel that nothing good can come from each other; or Muslims and Jews. And we can see how this kind of thinking determines much that happens on the domestic and international political scene. It is somehow easier to write other people off than to struggle to grow into the understanding of what their reality is and what it must be like to be them. Prejudice of this kind is widespread and, as such, will also have sown its seeds in us. And so we must be careful always to examine our own opinions, to remain open to their radical transformation; we must keep them before God and be prepared to sacrifice them whenever he will require. All too easily our opinions on things can become an absurd white elephant, cumbersome and no longer relevant, and yet for which we are prepared to fight tooth and nail.

But the greatest challenge of all to change and to grow is that which comes from our contact with other people. Nothing else can break down prejudice and smallness of being so effectively as first-hand experience of another person's reality. And so in all our contacts with other people, we need to remain radically open to them, and to God. We need to be prepared to say Yes to God at any moment if our assumptions and prejudices are challenged and if we are asked to go the healing (though generally painful!) way of personal growth.

Change and transformation are the very essence of our existence. And this is a law which we can experience dramatically in our spiritual living. However firm our intentions may be in one moment of time to love God with the whole of our being, we may find ourselves denying him in the next. Like St Peter, we can be embarrassed by our protestations of zeal. Or perhaps if we make some resolution to serve God better in a particular way, then we find that our good intentions founder: 'If we wish to stay awake in vigil, then we must sleep against our will, if we wish to fast, we must eat, if we wish to remain in silence and in peace, then things happen quite differently.' But, as John Tauler continues, all is not lost. This failure teaches us a deeper dependence on God: 'Thus every form of fixity is broken, and we are turned back upon our own nothingness, and are dependent upon God, acknowledging him in simple, humble faith and renouncing all fixity.'

From this changeability in our nature there springs the prayer of repentance. We are all prone to sin and to unauthentic forms of being, when we subordinate what is best in us to what is worst, and when we squander the preciousness of existence in forms of escape and indifference. The important thing when we fail in this way, as we all do, is not to fall into despair. Despair is yet another form of 'fixity'. It is to cling to one moment in time, to one way of being. It is to deny the transformational character of our own true nature. There can be no despair in the Kingdom of God, because there can be no fixity. All is movement there, and if we have fallen low, then we can rise again. If we are weak, then we can become strong.

We seem in today's society to have lost sight of the prayer of repentance. Perhaps this results from being told too much about our sinfulness in the past, so that acknowledging the uncertainty of our moral nature became a form of morbidity or a life-denying scrupulousness rather than healthy spiritual living. And yet a sense of sin is fundamental to a living relationship with God. And it is so because God himself gives us the sense of our own failings in order to deepen our life in him. Where we are spiritually complacent, God can find no place in us. Where we are unaware of and unconcerned about our failings, God cannot penetrate. We are most resistant to him, not where we sin but where we are indifferent to our sin. For guilt, conscience, the sense of our sin is itself a gift from God and it speaks of our deep orientation to him. To have no sense of sin, whether we are 'in' the Church or not, is to be outside the number of his people. And to have a sense of our failings is to be already in dialogue with him, who is the source of that unease and the one hope of its healing.

Repentance is a gift whereby we may bathe the whole of our being in the healing light of God's presence. This means not just the good parts of us but the bad ones too, those elements in us which are mediocre and indifferent. Repentance and confession is the way by which we attain a new wholeness in God, based not on selectivity and pretence, but on the real person which we are.

Change and transformation are the very essence of our existence. Consider our bodies, for instance. Their ageing is a process we all can ignore but none can avoid. The body, which is our own containing reality, grows, blossoms and withers away, like the flowers of the field. Death surrounds us like the sky.

Death is the circle that rings our existence, defining it and limiting it. It is the unscalable wall that tells us we can go no further. And yet, although we all know that 'one day' we will die, the full force of this truth only intermittently makes itself felt. The occasion is usually our own lucky escape from an accident, or the fate of others to whom we are close. Such is the effect of this reality we call death that we feel any system, any philosophy or religion which fails to take account of its powerful subterranean presence cannot be any more than traces on a surface. The death of our bodies defines who we are; it sets the limits beyond which we cannot go. It presents our natural being with the total and absolute finality of its own end. It is St Augustine who reminds us that death is the sole certainty. If we have faith, then we cannot know whether we will keep it; if we have no faith, we cannot know that we won't acquire it. If we are rich, we cannot know that we won't die poor, and if we are poor, we cannot know that we won't die rich. Nothing in life is certain, he tells us, but death alone. And even then we do not know how or when we will die, but only that death is our certain end.

Death is the permanent presence that grounds our life. But the curious fact remains that there is much in our culture which would seek to convince us that death does not (or need not) happen at all. People afflicted with serious illness often speak of their sense of 'shame'. It is socially awkward to be mortal. It is a 'wrong move' to die. The fear we all naturally have of death threatens to create a kind of mass hypnosis whereby we all live charmed lives and are faintly reproving of those 'weak-links' who 'fall by the wayside'. Of course, there are other more wholesome attitudes within our society, but all too often death becomes an area of private grief, a kind of solitary punishment cell into which we all from time to time are pushed. Since death seems an enormous all-powerful, all-destroying and utterly alien force in our own lives, we cannot imagine how anyone can ever come to terms with it, and so we banish it to the limits of consciousness where, if we are lucky, we can almost forget for long periods of time that it even exists.

But the timeless truth is that a life which is deeply authentic and beautiful with that particular kind of beauty which is the radiance of the spirit, must be lived within the very bowels of death. For unless we come to terms with that reality, which sometimes seems to us to be so much greater than our own, we will never live in a way which *matters*. Our living will be trivial and slight; our being will be shallow. Death, in all its awesome finality, must not be thought away or reduced. It must not be avoided or awareness of it suppressed. It is far too big and important a thing for us not to live towards it, with a life centred on our own mortality, in the joy, the love and the resoluteness which comes from the very deepest kind of being. Death is the other side of living, and we cannot drive it from our lives without losing something of the essence of what it means to be alive.

But how can we live in the presence, the very bowels, of death, without becoming depressed or numbed by its power? The answer is that we need to discover death as the very heart of transfiguration and of life. And death, for the Christian, is that with which we have a very special relation. We are after all baptized into the transformational death of Christ, and into his Life. Each time we say Yes to God, each time we live in and towards him rather than ourselves, we accept death into our experience. We live with death. We are transfigured. And, in the light of this constant inworking of God within us, the formation of our narrow, incomplete and hide-bound being into his own superabundant Life, the loving acceptance of our own death can be our greatest victory. Although it may be a far greater and more complete transformation than any-thing else we are likely to experience, although it is a transformation from what is known to what is only intuit-ively sensed, physical death can be a great – often our greatest – opportunity to love and to welcome God into the very heart of our being. Not all of us are called to be heroes of the faith or martyrs, but all of us face the ultimate challenge of our own physical disintegration. During our ordinary living we can easily deceive ourselves in all kinds of ways; but when our body is *in extremis* there is no place left for deception. All is bathed in the stark light of truth. And so, in this moment of our own deepest truth, we have the privilege of saying an almighty Yes to God, into the darkness, if there is darkness; into the suffering, if there is suffering; into the despair, if that is the truth of our being in that moment. And by saying Yes, we free ourselves ultimately to voyage forth out into his love.

Death, which is life, is the culmination and the crown of the existence of the believer. Our end is in extinction and resurrection, destruction and new birth. We cannot banish physical death to the margins, therefore, but we must learn through grace to love it and to trust it as the way that leads to God. And in an age which is so little concerned with Hell, we should not forget his promise of Heaven. For that is something we will all have felt at some time or other on our journey of faith, however dimly, however inarticulately: the fragrance of God, the sweetness of God, the living air of Paradise.

In many ways, Paradise is what this little book has been all about. After all, beauty, the ineffable beauty of Spirit that breaks through the toughest, darkest and bleakest forms of this world, is the very light of Paradise. And transfiguration: that has been the book's other theme. For the way to Paradise is not to be taken for granted. Only the beautiful can keep the company of the Beautiful, and it is a beauty we slowly gain by allowing God to fashion us in his own way: suffering him to draw out the beauty that hides within us, under so many layers of dirt, indifference and neglect.

We began this book with the image of a stained-glass window deep within us, which is the symbol of our true being. Whether our window will be radiant and glorious with the light which is life will depend on the extent to which we conform our life to God's; the extent to which we suffer the fire of his transforming being, as it burns and purifies us in the circumstances of our everyday living. Above all, it will depend on the extent to which we give a wholehearted and open Yes to God's glory, not in the future or in the past, but now, in this moment of time which for you, the reader, and for me, as I write these lines, is our sole reality.

QUESTIONS TO ASK OURSELVES

1   Am I prepared to grow and to develop and to change in my opinions on things?

2   Am I prepared to *become*: to allow God to change me from within?

3   Do I say Yes to the reality of my own death or do I shy away from it into comforting illusions?

4   Do I accept God's promise of Heaven?

5   Do I say Yes to the will of God in the present moment?

6   Do I choose to live a life that is filled with God's beauty?